GOD'S HEART
FOR YOUR HOME

Creating *a* Place *of* Everyday Ministry

Tracie Moss *&* Elizabeth Winn

God's Heart for Your Home:
Creating a Place of Everyday Ministry

by Elizabeth Winn and Tracie Moss

copyright ©2013 by Elizabeth Winn and Tracie Moss

Trade paperback ISBN: 978-1-9386244-0-7
Ebook ISBN: 978-1-9386244-1-4

Cover design by Martijn van Tilborgh

God's Heart for Your Home is also available on Amazon Kindle, Barnes & Noble Nook and Apple iBooks.

Published by Kudu Publishing / *KuduPub.com*

We dedicate this book to our two amazing husbands, Kevin Moss and Sean Winn.

We can honestly say we would never have attempted to write this book without their constant support and encouragement.

We are two blessed gals to have men who stand behind our ministry, praying for us, cheering us on and wanting God's best for us.

ACKNOWLEDGMENTS

Sean: Thank you for loving me the way you do. No one makes me feel more competent, beautiful, and cherished as you do. Thank you for the countless hours of work you have put into the technical side of Living Well. You always strive for excellence as you design our website, blog, and graphics. Tracie and I trust you immeasurably and appreciate how you support and love the ministry alongside us. And lastly, thank you for being a man who loves God with all your heart. Your obedience and devotion to the Father is what I love most about you. Thank you for keeping our family firmly rooted in faith by praying over us, for us, and with us. I love you with all my heart.

Taylor Winn: Thank you son, for supporting me and cheering me on as I have written this book. Your willingness to allow me to share some of your life experiences, has been so helpful and has made the book more relatable to everyone who reads it. I love how you are running after Jesus. Watching you grow in your walk with Him has awakened in me a desire to know Him even more. I can't wait to see all God has in store for your life! I love you very much.

Elin Winn: Thank you for being such a wonderful daughter and for supporting me as I have written this book. Because you allowed me to share some of your story, the testimony of God's grace and your example of surrendering to it, will touch so many lives. I love how you listen and obey the voice of God in your life. I see you growing into this beautiful, strong, Godly woman and it makes me so proud. Your love for Living Well Ministry means the world to me. My heart is excited to watch God's perfect plan unfold in your life. I love you very much.

Kevin: Twenty five years ago you captured my heart and I continually thank God for you. From that day you have had an unwavering belief in me and I am a better wife, mother, friend, and servant because of your support. Thank you for believing in Living Well and never giving up on the idea of us writing. I am so grateful for your service to our God, country and to our family. Thank you for growing spiritually with me, it has been such a great journey loving God and loving others alongside you!

Ashley Miles: I was very young when you entered our world and so unsure of myself as a mom. I am thankful for your sweet spirit and patience as I navigated the parenting world. Thank you for being one of my biggest cheerleaders in whatever I decide to do. Your support and prayers for Living Well have meant so much to me. I have loved watching you become a Godly wife and mother - you inspire me every day. You are clothed with strength and dignity and your children will someday rise and call you blessed. I love you and I'm honored to call you friend.

John Miles: Thank you for taking our sweet daughter and being the spiritual leader of your home. I am so grateful that God is the center of all that you do. Thank you for loving Ashley, Cole, and Gracie fully and for being such a Godly father. I love you.

Emma Moss: Thank you for teaching me, stretching me, and bringing such fun to our home. I love watching you grow in your own walk with God as you have entered junior high. I love how your heart is so tender toward Him and others. He has great things in store for you! Thank you for what you sacrifice for Living Well while I'm gone and writing. I love you.

Thank you Susan Tolleson, our book coach, for taking two gals who had never put pen to paper and helping us become writers in our own right. You made this most challenging process a wonderful adventure as you gently encouraged and pushed us to do our best. You helped keep the reader in the forefront and reminded us often of what they needed.

Thank you for walking this journey with us and for being more than a coach, but our friend as well.

Thank you to Kudu Publishing for accepting our project. Martijn and Andy, you have been encouraging and patient as you have walked us through this journey. We are grateful for the personal investment, countless emails and calls you all have given as we have learned this industry. We fully believe you were an answer to our prayers.

And to our heavenly Father....as usual, words cannot convey our gratefulness for your help and anointing as we have written. Along the way we have questioned why you chose us to write this message, but your still small voice was always there, calling us to finish the task. Lord, thank you for the gift of our friendship, for it is a beautiful representation of your love in both our lives. We are forever thankful for it.

Elizabeth Winn
Tracie Moss

December 2012

CONTENTS

Introduction

THE POWER OF HOME

"Love the Lord your God with all your heart and with all your soul and with all your strength. These commandments that I give you today are to be on your hearts. Impress them on your children. Talk about them when you sit at home and when you walk along the road, when you lie down and when you get up. Tie them as symbols on your hands and bind them on your foreheads. Write them on the doorframes of your houses and on your gates." — Deuteronomy 6:5-9

ONE NIGHT AFTER EATING a bowl of Cheerios, I (Elizabeth) was walking up two little steps leading into my kitchen when I tripped and fell, landing on my knees on the tile floor. My ceramic bowl careened across the kitchen floor, breaking into a million pieces.

My husband, Sean, came running from the basement and found me leaning over, holding my knees and groaning. He immediately knelt down, put his hands over mine, and began to pray for me. After he finished, I managed to get out the words, "I think I'm going to need some ice." As he went to the fridge, my teenage daughter, Elin, came into the kitchen and sat down next to me on the steps. She put an arm around my shoulders and asked if I was okay. I told her my knees were really hurting, so she put her other hand on them and began to pray. She asked God to drive out the pain and help my knees to stop hurting. Then she helped me over to our couch and Sean brought some ice.

As I sat there, I began to realize that even though my knees were throbbing, my heart was full. I felt very comforted and cared for. I began to realize I had just been ministered to. But it wasn't in any kind of formal way—I wasn't in church, at my weekly Bible study, my bi-monthly small group or a prayer meeting. I was just in my own home. My husband and daughter had simply ministered God's care, comfort and love to me.

The truth that God desires our homes to be places where His presence is welcomed, invited, and acknowledged above anything or anyone else began to take root inside of me. I realized how God longs for our homes to be where He is active, alive and allowed to touch us as we love and live together. I sensed just how much He wants our homes to be places of ministry.

The word "ministry" can mean different things to people. When Tracie and I took an informal survey of our friends and family, their responses varied widely.

Each definition was great, but our favorite was this: **"Ministry is allowing God's grace to manifest through our interactions with others."**

If our homes are to become places of ministry, then they must become places where God's grace is manifested through everyone living there. To our children, the home is the first place they experience this manifestation of God's grace, where they learn how to allow this grace to flow out of them to others. On the night I fell, I experienced the grace of God through Sean's and Elin's prayers and their tender care. It was beautiful.

Tracie and I believe this is God's desire for our homes. We have experienced life together since 1979 and shared many parenting joys and challenges. God brought us together in science class as seventh graders, and our love for God and each other has grown from there. As we have supported each other through marriage and parenting, we began to feel a burden for women and the drain we were seeing on them as believers, wives and mothers. We began Living Well Ministry to encourage, lift up, and challenge women to live a balanced life, full of Christ. Eventually, the idea for this book came from my experience and we both began to blog about "Ministry in the Home."

As this book has been written, we have used the term "we" unless one of us is sharing a personal story. Also, all scripture references are given with the New International Translation unless otherwise noted.

At the end of each chapter you will find reflection questions to help you apply or meditate on the truths that God has shared with you. Our hope is that you will find a group of women with whom to share this journey, as we know that support and encouragement are not only helpful, but biblical. God encourages us to "do life together" as He knew it would, at times, be tough.

Ecclesiastes 4:12: *"Though one may be overpowered, two can defend themselves. A cord of three strands is not quickly broken."*

Ecclesiastes 4:9: *"Two people are better off than one, for they can help each other succeed."*

Proverbs 27:17: *"As iron sharpens iron, so one person sharpens another."*

We believe godly parenting means going beyond providing just a "Christian" home for our children. We believe God wants our homes to be power-packed sanctuaries for our kids, where He is free to move and display His awesome power. We want our homes to be places of refuge, where the Holy Spirit is welcome to heal, comfort, encourage, protect and deliver.

The enemy is afraid of these kind of homes because he knows the residents are aware of his schemes and know how to fight. In these homes it's obvious, from the youngest to the oldest, God occupies every heart and all eyes are fixed on Him and His truth. This speaks of homes filled with activity rooted in God and His character.

It goes way beyond just families who believe in God, go to church, pray over their meals and try to live right. God's desire is for our homes to manifest His love in and through every member of our family. This is the power of a home!

A HOME OF PURPOSE

"But as for me and my household, we will serve the Lord."
— Joshua 24:15

HAVE YOU EVER WONDERED why God put His human creation into families? Malachi 2:15 (Amplified) explains it so well: *"And did not God make [you and your wife] one [flesh]? Did not One make you and preserve your spirit alive? And why [did God make you two] one? Because He sought a godly offspring [from your union]."* His purpose for our families is that we raise our children to love Jesus and serve Him and live for kingdom purposes.

We all are familiar with Joshua 24:15, *"As for me and my house, we will serve the Lord."* You may even have this verse displayed in your home somewhere. This scripture could very easily be the mantra in a house focused on living God's grace through ministry. But it's a focus we fear is becoming less and less evident in many Christian homes today.

Statistics suggest that three out of four Christian young people leave the church after graduating high school. This is tragic. Why are so many young people walking away from their faith? Could it be because they are not experiencing the demonstration of God's character, power and authority in their home? The church is not failing our kids, we are. The church only connects with our kids for an hour on Sunday. We are a daily influence on our kids. Make no mistake, God will hold us accountable for our efforts or lack of them in raising our children to love and obey Him. Our children will make their choices, but we must do our part to influence those choices.

> The church is not failing our kids, we are.

Of course, our number one goal for our children is they come to salvation, asking Jesus to forgive their sins and come live in their hearts. But our next goal needs to be for them to have a relationship with Jesus outside of us.

Eventually we want our children to live for the Lord and use their gifts to have influence on the world around them. In 2 Peter 1:5-8 we are encouraged:

"For this very reason, make every effort to add to your faith goodness; and to goodness, knowledge, and to knowledge, self control; and to self control, perseverance; and to perseverance, godliness, and to godliness, brotherly kindness; and to brotherly kindness, love. For if you possess these qualities in increasing measure, they will keep you from being ineffective and unproductive in your knowledge of our Lord Jesus Christ."

We desire for our children not just to get saved and have just enough Jesus to get them to heaven, but for them to be productive and effective in their knowledge of Him and His purpose for them on earth. When we begin to be purposeful in making our homes places of ministry—where God's grace is manifested—then our children begin to take on the nature and heart of Jesus. Who doesn't want that for their kids?

So how do we go about creating this kind of environment in our homes?

Be Intentional

We have to be intentional about our actions and reactions if we're going to create an environment of ministry in our homes; it won't just happen. We set the tone for the day, for the activity, for the interaction, and for the love and care that takes place. In essence, we are God's hands and feet to our spouse and children. We need to model His love, grace, compassion, servant's heart, encouragement, and to be His arms and hands that hold our loved ones in times of trouble. Proverbs 3:27 (MSG) says, *"Never walk away from someone who deserves help; your hand is God's hand for that person."*

> We are God's hands and feet to our spouse and children.

Now that sounds like a ton of responsibility, doesn't it? The good news is, we can't and don't have to do this on our own. Really, only God can help us through this journey. We can make all the plans, create the best lists, set all the boundaries, decide on all the ways we are going to parent, but if we don't place all of it at the foot of the cross, we set ourselves up for disappointment and unnecessary struggles. He has promised to come alongside us and guide us, but we first have to give it to Him. Proverbs 16:9 (MSG) tells us *"We plan the way we want to live, but only God makes us able to live it."*

He wants us to seek Him first in all things and especially with something as precious as our families. Creating an environment where He is the head takes intentional planning. It requires a daily surrender of our control and a heart that is eager to listen for the leading of the Holy Spirit. This kind of heart will create the loving environment of ministry to our family and all those who enter our homes. And it will set the example of how we expect our family to treat one another and others.

One way I (Tracie) do this is when the alarm clock goes off. Before my feet hit the floor, I quickly whisper a prayer,

"Lord, today is yours, please guide and direct me and use me in every interaction." He promises that He is attentive to our requests and He enjoys supporting His children!

So, what should we be intentional about?

Making God the center of the home

Before anything else, we must place God in His rightful place at the center of our homes. They should be the platform to promote Jesus intentionally throughout the day—woven through every interaction. This is clearly spelled out in Deuteronomy 6:4-9:

> *"Love the Lord your God with all your heart and with all your soul and with all your strength. These commandments that I give you are to be on your hearts. Impress them on your children. Talk about them when you sit at home and when you walk along the road, when you lie down and when you get up. Tie them as symbols on your hands and bind them on your foreheads. Write them on your doorframes of your houses and on your gates."*

Creating an atmosphere like this doesn't happen with a once-a-week trip to church. It happens through continual conversations where He is the main topic, the Word is quoted, God is consulted, and He is ever-present. Jesus should be given His proper place as a name of praise and thanksgiving and never as a curse word or blamed for circumstances. Modeling this attitude in our own life is so important for our children to see. Do you portray Him as your personal God, counselor, guide, Father, healer, comforter, and compass?

The passage from Deuteronomy encourages us to "talk about them (scriptures or commandments) when you sit at home and when you are out, when you lie down and when you get up." This basically means all the time!

When something good happens, acknowledge Him by saying, "Thank you, Jesus!" When you or someone in the family is sad or hurting, go to the Word for guidance and solace. When your child has questions or they are looking to you for guidance, your response could be, "Well, let's see what the Word has to say about that." Then go and look it up together, write the scriptures down and place them where your children can see them throughout their day.

When you compliment your children or want to encourage them, use the Word that never returns void. Speak the Word over them as a blessing, such as Genesis 1:27, "You are made in His image," and Psalm 139:14, "You are fearfully and wonderfully made" and a "delight to Him."

What does this look like in everyday life? Here are some ideas for making God the center of your home:

- Hang or post scriptures or words of encouragement around the home—even on your "doorframes."

- Place scriptures on your mirror or those of your children so they can read words of encouragement while getting ready in the morning and before bed.

I (Tracie) did this when my daughter Emma went through a time where she was having horrible dreams and was fearful to go to bed at night. We went to the Word and found several scriptures about "God's love casting out fear" (1 John 4:18) and not being "anxious about anything, but by prayer and supplication make your requests known to God and the peace that passes all understanding will be yours" (Phil. 4:6). We wrote the verses on sticky notes and posted them on her bathroom mirror. While she was brushing her teeth at night, we would read over every one of those scriptures and then pray them over her just as we were turning off the lights. God's Spirit rested on her and she was much more at peace about going to bed.

- When you are walking or driving with your children, make notice of the beauty of God's workmanship—thank Him for the color of the trees or the sunrise.

- When you are at the dinner table, choose conversation starters that lend themselves to Him being at the center, such as, "What are two things you are thankful for today?," or, "How were you used or blessed today?"

- In the morning when you rise, have a quiet time or a particular place for prayer and reading.

- Have a short devotion with your children and/or spouse to begin the day with a godly perspective.

- In the evening, write in a gratitude journal or talk with your children about the blessings of the day.

- When you put your children to bed, pray with them specifically about who God is to them, the protection He provides, His grace, and what a gift they are from Him.

Incorporating any of these interactions in our daily lives will allow our children to see the importance God has in our lives, and He will look attractive and approachable. This intentional placing of God in His proper place will establish the priority of having Him as the integral center of our homes.

Realizing God knows better than I do what my child needs

I (Elizabeth) have always been pretty black-and-white when it comes to behavior and discipline. I didn't think too much about my reactions when my kids made a poor choice—I doled out the appropriate consequence and we went on. But God showed me the error in my thinking through an experience with my daughter, Elin.

During the summer before Elin's junior year of high school, we felt God calling us to homeschool her. She was walking through a very difficult time in her life and struggling with depression. We had not dealt with depression up close, so this was new for all of us. We were trying our best to meet her needs, but quite frankly we were in unknown territory. It was a prime place for God to teach us some valuable lessons.

One morning, Elin woke up feeling really down. I had been trying to get her to eat something before starting her school work, but she was being very difficult to converse with. Frustrated, I suggested she go into the dining room to start her work. I was left at the kitchen sink rinsing some dishes when the Holy Spirit spoke to my heart.

"I want you to go hold Elin," I heard. I chuckled and said right back, *"Lord, perhaps you haven't noticed, but Elin doesn't seem to want anything to do with me this morning."* I walked into our laundry room and the Holy Spirit spoke again, *"Elizabeth, I want you to go hold Elin."* Again I argued. *"Lord, she does not want me to hold her!"* I went back to the kitchen and again was nudged by the Holy Spirit. With a bit more intensity He said, *"Elizabeth, go hold Elin."*

I finally relented. I went into the dining room and said, "Elin, come over here for a minute." She got up. "Come sit with me on the couch. I feel the Holy Spirit wants me to hold you." She came and sat next to me, leaning into my arms. It wasn't two seconds before she was crying and I was, too. I just sat there holding her and praying over her. After about ten minutes she sat up, wiped her eyes, got up and went back to the dining room table. I was left thinking, "Okay, that went well, I guess."

That night as I was getting into bed, I found a note from Elin on my pillow. She had written:

Mom, today has been a pretty awful day, but you made it better and I just wanted to say thank you for that. Sitting with you and hugging you earlier today meant the world to me. I don't know what I would do without you. Mom, I don't know what's wrong with me. I feel tired and hopeless and I just want to be Elin again.

God spoke again to me: *"Elizabeth, Elin needed Me to hold her today and your arms were the only arms avail-*

able to use. Please understand that I always know what she needs; you don't."

I learned so much from this experience. First, God is the only one who really knows what our kids need at any given moment. We may think we know, but much of the time we don't.

Second, we must learn to stop and listen for—and obey—His voice. Since He knows what they need, we must learn to recognize His voice and hear what we need to do or how we need to respond so His will can be done. It's not easy; many of us struggle so much with stopping and listening. It's hard to put aside our opinions and thoughts and be still long enough to hear His thoughts.

> **God is the only one who really knows what our kids need at any given moment.**

One time, Elin was very angry with God. She did not understand why He was allowing certain things to happen in her life. She was angry and questioning His existence and I found myself mad. I did not stop and listen to God. I went into defense mode and reacted to Elin instead of responding to her.

"What do you mean is God even real?" I fumed. "Are you serious? How can you even think that! Look at all He has done for you and our family! How can you doubt His love for you?" Yes, I know: wrong reaction. As you can imagine, this did not help Elin. In fact it angered her more.

Later in the day as I was praying about it, God spoke to my heart. *"Elizabeth, I am okay with Elin being angry with Me, I can handle it. I don't need you to defend Me."* I wish I had stopped and listened to Him instead of launching into my little tirade.

I have also learned that people sometimes "need" what they don't "deserve." The morning she wouldn't eat breakfast, Elin deserved to be left by herself. But God knew she needed something completely different than what she deserved. She needed comfort and love and a touch from Him. My time of holding her did much more for her than being left alone.

When we respond to God's prompting to give our kids what they need over what they might deserve, we give God the opportunity to open their eyes to His truth. An example of this was when, as a young teen, Elin made a choice that was deserving of major discipline and consequence. She was sorrowful and repentant, and knew she deserved to be punished. Sean and I told her we needed some time to pray and talk over her consequence. The next day, he and I got together after praying separately. God had spoken to both of us that what Elin needed was grace. No punishment. We knew it didn't make a lot of sense, and quite frankly wondered what God was up to.

As we sat down with Elin, I could tell she was prepared for whatever consequence we were about to hand down. When Sean told her we felt God was telling us to extend her grace and not punishment, she began to weep. Her response was so telling, "But I deserve to be punished!" We told her we knew that, but God knew she needed grace. She walked away from the experience changed, as she saw first-hand what grace looked and felt like.

In the following pages we are going to talk about the different avenues ministry can take. Whether in prayer, encouragement, forgiveness, or taking ministry outside our home, it all begins with remembering that for ministry to take place, we have to be mindful of it and purposeful in creating an environment where ministry can thrive.

As Jesus is welcomed and invited into our homes daily, He will become active and alive in each of the hearts who live there. His voice will become more and more recognizable as we go to Him for His knowledge of what our kids need.

You may feel as though it's too late for you to establish an environment of ministry in your home, as your kids are already teens or are out of the house. But be assured, it's never too late to begin making the changes necessary for God to be welcomed and invited into your home.

And if you are a grandparent, what a wonderful heritage to leave for your grandchildren, to know that when they come to grandma and grandpa's house, they will meet Jesus and see His power in action through prayer, encouragement, forgiveness, and ministry to others.

Reflection Questions

1. We asked several friends and family members what "ministry" meant to them. What does it mean to you?

2. When you think of a "Christian" home, what characteristics come to mind?

3. What are your thoughts when we say that God wants our families to experience more than just a "Christian" home? Do you agree?

4. What are you doing to be intentional about making Jesus the center of your home?

5. What could you start doing today to bring Jesus to a more prominent place in your home?

6. What are your thoughts on God knowing more than you do what your kids need?

7. Can you think of a time when you should have stopped, prayed and listened when dealing with your child, instead of moving out and acting on your own?

8. Has your child ever needed something different than what they deserved?

9. What are your fears or concerns as you begin to move forward to create an environment for ministry in your home?

10. Reflecting on your childhood home environment, what are the key elements you would choose to bring into your home and what are the ones you would leave in the past?

Spend time in prayer and ask the Holy Spirit to open your mind and heart to creating this type of atmosphere in your home. Perhaps tell Him:

Dear Lord,

Please make our home a dwelling place for Your presence. I desire my home to be more than just a "Christian" home. I want it to be a place where You are alive and active in everyone living here. I open up my heart to listen and respond as You speak to me and guide me in taking steps to creating an environment in my home where ministry can take place.

Help my home to be a refuge and sanctuary for my children and may our family have great impact for Your kingdom.

2
A HOME OF PRAYER

"The prayer of a righteous man is powerful and effective."

— James 5:16

IN HIS EARTHLY LIFE, Jesus set the example for the importance of prayer. He made a point to meet with His Father every day through prayer. If Jesus couldn't fulfill His purpose on earth without praying, we can't even begin to fulfill ours without it.

Prayer is not an optional extra in the life of a Christ follower. If we are going to grow in our relationship with Jesus and lead our children in relationship with Him, we need prayer as a source of power and wisdom in our lives. In order to create an atmosphere of ministry in our homes, everyone needs to understand how important prayer is and be comfortable praying beyond just blessing our food.

Pray out loud - So the dewil Can hear it.

Prayer changes things. It alters hearts, minds, attitudes, and the atmosphere in our homes. Prayer gives God the opportunity to speak. When we spend time in prayer, we can invite the Holy Spirit to be part of everything that goes on in our homes. God's character dwells among us when He is invited to come in and saturate our homes. His peace, love, patience, kindness, and gentleness surround us and our children (Gal. 5:22-23). When Jesus becomes such a large part of the atmosphere of our homes, ministry will naturally follow.

No one would argue our need for God's help as we parent our children and lead them in a relationship with Jesus. The enemy uses the world's culture to constantly steal the seed we are planting in our children's hearts. As we are working to produce "fruit bearers" for God's kingdom, the enemy wants nothing more

> **The enemy wants nothing more than to pull our children into his clutches.**

than to pull our children into his clutches. Psalm 121 is a declaration we can count on as we seek God's help in our role as parents:

> *"I lift my eyes to the hills, where does my help come from? My help comes from the Lord, the Maker of heaven and earth. He will not let your foot slip, He who watches over you will not slumber; indeed He who watches over Israel will neither slumber nor sleep. The Lord watches over you, the Lord is your shade at your right hand; the sun will not harm you by day nor the moon by night. The Lord will keep you from all harm, He will watch over your life; the Lord will watch over your coming and going both now and forevermore."*

As parents, we can declare this powerful psalm as God's promise to be our help and covering as we aim to be the best parents we can.

Praying the Word over our children

When my kids were young, I (Elizabeth) didn't spend very much time praying for them. It wasn't until they got older that I became more aware of the great need to pray over their lives. Notice "over," not "for." There is a difference. Praying "for" our kids is asking God for blessing and favor, which are wonderful things to ask for. But praying "over" our kids is more about protection and speaking into their life the character of Christ.

In parenting our kids, we need to be alert to the enemy and his tactics. We don't want him to get a stronghold in our children's lives. So this is where praying "over" them comes into play. When we pray "over" our kids, we are taking our place as the spiritual authority in their lives. We stand in front of them as a shield and protector, alerting the enemy that he will have to get through us first before touching them. It's a defensive posture in prayer with a warrior mentality.

Praying the Word over our children is one of the most powerful tools we have in our parenting arsenal against the enemy. Hebrews 4:12 says, *"For the word of God is **living** and **active**. Sharper than any double-edged sword, it penetrates even to dividing soul and spirit, joints and marrow; it judges the thoughts and attitudes of the heart."*

We can't go wrong using God's Word in prayer over our children's lives. The Bible does what it says it will do. There is nothing more effective than speaking scripture in faith out loud. The enemy hates it when we catch this revelation because he has no defense against it. We always win when we take God's Word and use it as a weapon against the enemy. This is the best thing we can do when we pray, especially when we are not sure what our children need.

> **There is nothing more effective than speaking scripture in faith out loud.**

Here are a few scriptures I often pray over Taylor and Elin:

- "Lord, I thank you that Taylor and Elin are God's workmanship, created in Christ Jesus to do good works, which God prepared in advance for them to do." (Eph. 2:10).

- "Lord, I thank you that Taylor and Elin will flee the evil desires of youth, and pursue righteousness, faith, love and peace, along with those who call on the Lord out of a pure heart." (2 Tim. 2:22).

- "I thank you, Jesus, that no weapon formed against Taylor or Elin today will prosper in the name of Jesus!" (Isa. 54:17).

Praying protection over our children

Another part of praying over our kids is to pray protection over them. The Word is very clear that the devil is like a thief, trying to kill, steal and destroy us (John 10:10). He is so hungry for our kids that one of our top priorities should be protecting them, through prayer. God solidified this truth in me a few years ago, when Taylor was in the middle of seventh grade.

It was a new environment for him as he was used to a small Christian school in Texas, and this was a very large public school in a new community. As I dropped him off one morning, I spoke out loud as I watched him walk into school, "Lord, I feel as though I'm dropping him off in a war zone." The Lord answered, *You are. But if you pray over him, I will protect him.*

All of a sudden God gave me a vision of the hallway in Taylor's school. Kids were walking up and down the hall while above them were hideous, black, winged demons flying back and forth. Once in a while one would swoop down and land on one of the kids, who would fall under the weight. Some kids had a demon hanging off their backs, weighing them down. Then I noticed Taylor coming down the hallway.

Surrounding him on all sides were four magnificent, huge, powerful, warring angels. They were very aware of the demons, watching them as their hands rested on giant swords hanging off the belts at their waists. If one of the demons would take a lunge at Taylor, the angels immediately reacted and pulled out their swords and sliced away. The creature would cry out and slink off wounded.

This insight drastically changed the way I prayed over my kids. I began to get very specific in praying protection over them. Here are four areas I pray daily over Taylor and Elin:

1. I ask God to put a hedge of protection and to place angels around them according to Psalms (91:11).

2. I ask God to give them wisdom beyond their years as they face different situations (Prov. 2).

3. I ask God to draw them by His Holy Spirit into relationship with Him. I ask that He would pour into them a desire for the Word and a desire to spend time with Him in prayer. I pray for Jesus to become the lover of their souls.

4. I ask God to help them recognize His voice and to recognize evil; we can't always be with them to protect them, but God is always with them.

An answer to this last prayer came one time when Elin was in fifth grade. Her Girl Scout troop was playing a levitation game at one of their meetings. Elin knew something was not right. She didn't know why, but she did not want to play so she asked to leave the room. When Elin got in the car, she broke down in tears and told me what had happened. I encouraged her that what she felt was from the Holy Spirit, who was helping her to recognize evil. I prayed over her, told the enemy he had no power over her, and then rebuked a spirit of fear. Elin settled down and was fine.

We must remember that just because we can't see the supernatural world, this does not mean it doesn't exist. I am so thankful for the vision God gave me of the demonic activity in Taylor's school. I had not thought of his environment in those terms, but once I saw what reality was, it ignited in me a passion to pray. It helps to envision what God's protection does for your children. If you could have seen the size of the angels in my vision, believe me, you would be asking God to send angels to protect your child! It also serves as a constant reminder to go to God for protection on behalf of our children.

It's never too late to begin praying over our children. The beautiful thing about prayer is we can do it anytime, anywhere. As long as we have breath, we can pray. It is comforting to know that if we lost all our abilities to do anything, we could still pray over our kids. We could still be powerful parents and have tremendous impact on their lives. James 5:16 (KJV) promises that *"the effectual fervent prayer of a righteous man avails much."* This is the kind of praying parents we need to be!

The power of the Holy Spirit in our child's life

Another important aspect of prayer is allowing the Holy Spirit, through prayer, to change our child's heart in a way we never can. It may be an attitude, habit or pattern of behavior that does not honor God, or it may be an attribute of their character we'd like to see flourish.

As my children grew older, I (Elizabeth) noticed my "lectures" were having less and less impact. One day as I finished up one of those "lectures and suggestions," the Holy Spirit spoke to my heart: *"Elizabeth, I need you to be quiet. I can't speak to your kids if you are always talking."*

That hurt. But as I began to be quiet and allow the Holy Spirit to speak to my child, change happened. I learned that our kids can't hear God's voice if we're always talking.

> **Our kids can't hear God's voice if we're always talking.**

I have found the Holy Spirit to be much more effective in reaching my children's hearts than I ever could be.

Our kids need to learn to recognize the voice of the Holy Spirit. We should encourage them to seek God when they walk through a difficult time, have questions, or need direction. It's tempting for us as parents to try answering the questions for them, or telling them what we think. But when we direct them to find out for themselves what God is saying, they learn what God's voice sounds like in their life, which will produce a desire to keep their relationship with Him strong and intact. We ultimately want our children's hearts to cry out like Psalm 73:25-28:

> "Whom have I in heaven but you? And earth has nothing I desire besides you. My flesh and my heart may fail, but God is the strength of my heart and my portion forever. Those who are far from you will perish; you destroy all who are unfaithful to you. But as for me, it is good to be near God, I have made the Sovereign Lord my refuge; I will tell of all your deeds."

Here are some suggestions on how you can encourage your kids to learn to discern God's voice:

- Talk to them about having a "secret place" of prayer, a special place for them to go when they want to talk to God. Let them choose this special space.

- When they are troubled about something, after praying with them, encourage them to go to their "secret place" to spend time with God, asking Him to speak to them.

- Give them a journal and encourage them to write down what they hear God saying to them or draw a picture about what they are hearing.

- Write down a simple Bible verse and ask them to spend time reading it, meditating on it and listening to see what God speaks to them about it. Have them write about it in their journal.

- For older kids, ask them often what they are reading in their Bible and what God is saying to them. This tells them you expect them to be nurturing their own relationship with God.

- When your older kids are going through difficulty, keep in close connection with them by praying with them, but also ask them what they hear God saying.

Praying with our children

Praying over our children during our own quiet times or when they are not present is vital, but it's also good for them to hear us pray with them using the Word.

The Word is so incredibly powerful and is exactly what we need when we need it: sharp, soothing, healing, or convicting. When we speak it over our children, they learn its content, how to trust it, and how powerful and active it is to affect lives. When we pray with our children using the Word, we should be detailed about our requests. Being specific in our prayers shows our children that the Bible has the answer for anything that comes their way.

> Being specific in our prayers shows our children that the Bible has the answer for anything that comes their way.

I (Tracie) like to place my child's name in the scripture; this way they hear the Word spoken over them and it becomes personal to their life and situation.

Here are a few examples of detailed prayers:

For sickness:

- "Lord, you have said that we are healed by your stripes (Isaiah 53:5), and that we can come to you in your name, so we ask that (their name) is healed by your stripes."

- "You said that we are wonderfully made and in Your image (Genesis 1:27), so we ask that every part of (_____'s) body is exactly as You formed it and it is working just as you knit her/him together (Psalm 139:13)."

- "I pray, Jesus, that power goes out from you and heals (_____) (Luke 6:19)."

For anxiety or fear:

- "I pray that (_____) receives the peace that you, Jesus, have left with her/him, the peace you gave to her/him. Let not her/his heart be troubled, neither let it be afraid (John 14:27)."

- "I pray that You, Lord, are my (_____'s) helper and that she/he will not fear (Hebrews 13:6)."

For Correction:

- "Lord, I pray that (_____) will be quick to hear, slow to speak and slow to anger so her/his righteousness will come forth (James 1:19)."

- "I pray, Lord, that (_____) loves You and keeps Your commandments (John 14:15)."

For Confidence:

- "I pray that (_____) realizes that in all these things she/he is more than a conqueror through You who loved her/him(Romans 8:37)."

- "Lord, I pray that (_____) will be confident of this very thing, that You who have begun a good work in her/him will complete it until the day of Jesus Christ (Philippians 1:6)."

Over the years, I (Tracie) have kept a prayer journal for many of the prayers for my children. When I'm praying about a particular situation, I will write a brief note and date the prayer. I love to look back and see how God answered our prayers. At various times in my life, or in the lives of my children, I have needed a reminder of God's listening ear, and all I have to do is pick up that small book and review all the times He moved on our behalf. I also love to have my kids read through it periodically to see the notes I made and where God heard our prayers for them. This makes God very real to them.

When we use the Word to ask the Father specifically about our needs before we do anything else, it puts Him where He belongs—in authority over our bodies and circumstances. So when we pray with our children, they learn the Word and begin to understand that God is the head of our lives and every circumstance we encounter.

As my kids entered their late teen years, Sean and I (Elizabeth) realized we needed to teach them to begin managing their own lives through prayer. Up to this point, we had done the spiritual warfare in their lives when we saw the enemy attack. We stood up and fought for them, laying our hands on them and rebuking the enemy. But we realized as they grew older and began to carve out their own relationship with God, they needed to learn to draw their *own* swords and fight the enemy on their *own* behalf.

We began to talk to them about "earning a reputation with the devil." The devil learns, by our response to his attack, if we are easy prey or not. We let the enemy know we are not easy prey when we put on the armor of God (Eph. 6:10-17), and when we understand the devil cannot read our minds, therefore he only knows what effect he is having by what comes out of our mouth. So when he attacks, we attack right back with the Word as our sword, letting him know we recognize him and we will not relent. When we respond in this manner, we earn a reputation with him that we are not to be messed with and *if* he chooses to attack, he better be prepared to walk away bloody.

A recent example of this occurred when Elin came to me discouraged because someone had thrown in her face a mistake she had made in her past, trying to make her feel as though she had not changed and was still the same person as before. She was feeling frustrated and not understanding why her past mistakes kept coming up and asking herself, "Will anyone ever see me different?"

It was obvious to me the enemy had moved in and was trying to beat her up. I knew in that moment I could stand up and fight this battle for her; in fact, I really wanted to. It made me mad that the enemy thought he could mess with my kid. But I knew Elin had to fight this on her own. After talking to her a bit, I pointed out the enemy's involvement and how this was his attempt to discourage her, depress her, and pull her away from what God was doing in her life.

I could tell by her response she knew what I was talking about. I went on to encourage her to "earn that reputation" and respond herself to the enemy by letting him know he could not throw her past in her face, and that her past was under the blood of Jesus and she would not listen to his lies. I reminded her that the tone of her voice needed to represent the authority God had given her over the devil. In other words, she shouldn't say it nicely!

You may read this and feel as though you don't have the kind of reputation with the enemy you would like to have, so how can you teach your kids to "earn" this reputation. Be encouraged. We don't have to be perfect in managing our own prayer lives as we teach our kids how to manage theirs. God will give us wisdom along the way so as our kids begin to take responsibility of their own lives in prayer, they can do so with confidence because they have been under our wings and listened as we have prayed consistently with them their whole lives.

Going to God first

By creating an atmosphere of ministry in our homes, our children witness what faith looks like in our lives. Through our actions and reactions, our children see that God is our source for everything and they begin to encounter the peace and calm that His presence and the Word can provide, even in the craziest of situations.

Since prayer is such a powerful tool, it should be the first recourse when trouble or sickness comes. What is your first thought or action when someone gets hurt or needs help in your home? Is it typically chaos that spirals out of control, or is your home a place of peace and action?

- Have you created an atmosphere where your children believe God is big enough for some situations but not big enough for all?

- If Dad loses his job, can God be your source?

- If Mom is diagnosed with a life-threatening illness, can God be the healer?

- When a child is having trouble with friends, is God your comforter and help in times of need?

Our job is to help our children understand and watch as we place God in the rightful position as Lord of everything. Philippians 4:6-7 states: *"Do not be anxious about anything but in everything, by prayer and petition, with thanksgiving, present your requests to God. And the peace of God, which transcends all understanding, will guard your hearts and your minds in Christ Jesus."*

During times of trouble, He should be the first one we call, not our friends. In 1 Peter 5:7, we are encouraged to *"cast all our cares on Him for He cares for us."* The Word tells us that in all things we can go to the Father for guidance and help, and when we do the result is peace that we cannot comprehend. This type of peace is from the "Comforter" through the Holy Spirit. Everything can be spiraling out

> During times of trouble, He should be the first one we call, not our friends.

of control but you and your family will encounter a sense of calm and reassurance that will override the chaos.

As my oldest daughter, Ashley, began junior high I (Tracie) was given a book of scriptures that were categorized by need. When she would encounter a situation where she needed prayer, I would write next to that particular scripture the request and put the date. Then I would pray the Word over that situation and wait expectantly for an answer. One year when Ashley was home on summer break from college, she was having a difficult time in several areas of her life and really looking for direction. I pulled out that book and asked her to take some time to read through my prayers from a span of about eight years and see God's faithfulness and His hand in every area of her life. When she came out of that quiet time she was a new person, full of hope and encouragement. It is good for our children to see that He is constant, His word is powerful and it is exactly what they need for any situation.

This idea of "prayer first" is a habit that you may not have thought about before, or one that was not modeled for you as a child. It will take time and perseverance to create a mindset of communicating with the Father first, and then taking action. How do we change our mindset? 2 Corinthians 10:5 explains: *"We demolish arguments and every pretension that sets itself up against the knowledge of God, and we take captive every thought to make it obedient to Christ."*

If your "go-to" response is to run to the medicine cabinet or a person or into a tailspin over your circumstances, then you will need a plan. Ask the Holy Spirit to assist you in creating a new attitude of "Him first" and then to order your footsteps as to what the next action should be. This will take time and perseverance, but the results will be profound and your prayers will have a generational effect in your family.

God is worthy to be praised

Another component of a home focused on ministry is that it is a home of praise—giving God the honor and glory He deserves. Just like prayer, praise should be a regular activity—one that comes first in our thoughts and is spoken throughout the day. Our children are watching to see if what we say in prayer and on Sunday morning is real and authentic throughout the week. If He really is the center of our lives, do we continually praise Him? Here are a few scriptures to remind you of the praise that should be pouring out of us throughout the day:

- *"...from the rising of the sun to the place where it sets, the name of the Lord is to be praised."* (Ps. 113:3).

- *"I will proclaim the name of the Lord. Oh, praise the greatness of our God!"* (Deut. 32:3).

- *"I will sing to the Lord all my life; I will sing praise to my God as long as I live."* (Ps. 104:33).

- *"I will bless you Lord at all times. Your praise shall continually be in my mouth."* (Ps. 34:1).

At all times, as long as we live, continually... from the rising of the sun until it sets... remember Him when you rise, and when you walk along the road, and when you sit in your home, and so on. When our homes ring of these scriptures day and night, the enemy has no ground to slip in. Remember, the enemy has to flee when the name of the Lord is spoken (James 4:7)! That's the kind of powerful thinking you want your children leaving the house with every day.

One way I (Tracie) like to help myself and our family in this area of continual praise is to have scriptures and encouraging messages displayed throughout the house. Some are on plaques, some are framed, and others I just write on a plate in our kitchen. This goes along with Deuteronomy 11:19, where it tells us to speak of God's commandments and love throughout the day, and to post them on our doorframes and gates. This is just one way of keeping the Lord at the forefront of our minds.

This "praise first" attitude may also be something that was not modeled for you as a child and will take some practice. Over time, this will become your "go-to" action when something happens in your home or with your children, and eventually your children will begin to exhibit an attitude of praise in all things. I love when Emma comes to me in excitement, and the first thing out of her mouth is, "Thank you Jesus!" before she tells me what happened. I just smile and praise the Lord that she has absorbed the atmosphere that He is our center and deserves continual praise.

What prayer looks and sounds like

Whether we like it or not, our children learn about prayer primarily from watching and listening to us. If this strikes terror in your heart, please take comfort in remembering that prayer is simply talking to God. Praying out loud is no different than talking to our spouse or best friend. God desires us to be ourselves when we come to Him in prayer; we don't have to be

> Our children learn about prayer primariliy from watching and listening to us.

concerned about impressing Him. He wants us to relate to Him as though He is our best friend in the whole world. We don't have to sound spiritual or use special words when we pray. In fact, if we sound different than we usually do when we pray, our children will think they can't be themselves when they pray.

For our children to become comfortable with praying, it is imperative they have an example to follow. Children will basically mimic what they hear. An example of this was when I (Elizabeth) took the kids, without Sean, to see my folks. As I pulled out of the driveway, I asked Taylor, who was six at the time, if he would pray over our trip. He began to pray:

> *"Dear Lord, I just pray you would protect us as we go. Plead your blood over our car and camp angels everywhere around us. Help all the parts to work. In Jesus' name, Amen."*

I smiled as he prayed because he sounded just like Sean. Why? Because Taylor had observed Sean when he prayed over trips in the past, and he was mimicking what he had heard. Why do you think Elin, when she prayed over my hurt knees, asked Jesus to drive out pain? Because Sean or I have prayed many times over her, asking God to drive sickness out of her body.

When our children see and hear us pray, it gives them permission to pray, too. They realize they have a voice with God, as well. Praying helps our kids establish their own relationship with God and learn that not only can mom or dad approach God, but they can too.

Becoming comfortable with prayer

Prayer is a vital component of a ministering home. When our home is full of prayer, our children become very comfortable with it. They live with an assurance that, if and when trouble comes, God can and will help them. They also become more sensitive to the voice of the Holy Spirit and what He sounds like. Because of this, they recognize a need in someone's life and can use prayer to bring comfort to that person.

One time a lady in our church approached me with tears in her eyes. She told me how Elin had prayed with her the week before. Evidently, she had told Elin she was feeling a little sad about missing family, and Elin asked if she could pray for her. This lovely lady was touched by the ministry of prayer through Elin.

When we teach our children what prayer looks and sounds like, we are giving them a tool to take out into their world to minister the love of Christ to others. Our kids are surrounded by a world that is in desperate need of Jesus and His love. By understanding prayer, our children don't feel helpless when they encounter someone in need. They've seen the power of prayer in action, and are not afraid to step out and use it.

A house built on the Rock

When our homes are houses of prayer, they become the homes that Jesus talks about in Matthew 7:24: *"Therefore everyone who hears these words of mine and puts them into practice is like a wise man who built his house on the rock. The rain came down, the streams rose and the winds blew and beat against that house; yet it did not fall, because it had its foundation on the rock."*

Jesus is that rock we put our faith in as a family. Making prayer a priority in our homes gives our children a sense of security and peace so that when the storms of life hit our family's home, they know God is our Strong Tower, and that when we run to Him, our family is going to be safe (Prov. 18:10).

There is not enough money in the world to purchase that kind of peace and security for our kids. God will honor the home that puts prayer before everything else (2 Chron. 7: 14-16). Although making prayer a priority in our homes requires great intention on our part, it's worth it to see the power of God at work in and through our children's lives.

Reflection Questions

1. Reflect on your childhood home environment. What areas are you bringing into your home and what have you left behind? Why?

2. Take an honest assessment of your personal prayer life. What changes might God be asking you to make in order for your prayer life to become more powerful and effective?

3. What are your thoughts on the difference between praying "for" your kids as opposed to praying "over" them?

4. What was your reaction to the vision of Taylor's school? Could you visualize that scene? Did the thought of it scare you or empower you?

5. Do you find yourself "talking" too much and not giving your kids the opportunity to hear what the Holy Spirit is saying to them?

6. What ideas could you add to the list of ways to encourage your child to listen and hear from God?

7. What kind of reputation have you earned with the enemy?

8. Is the habit in your house to go to God first when trouble comes?

9. How important is the concept of "praise" in your home? Do you often praise God in front of your kids or lead them in praising God for who He is, or for answered prayer?

10. What is your comfort level in praying out loud? Are your kids experiencing a good example in your home of what prayer looks and sounds like?

3
A HOME OF ENCOURAGEMENT

"With each of you we were like a father with his child, holding your hand, whispering encouragement, showing you step-by-step how to live well before God, who called us into his own kingdom, into this delightful life." – 1 Thessalonians 2:11-12 (MSG)

THIS SCRIPTURE BRINGS TO MIND a calm father, affectionately holding on to his child, leaning in to whisper good things, and slowly, methodically guiding his child toward a Christ-filled life. Assisting our children to navigate this world and live well before God can be a daunting task, requiring much prayer and planning.

1 Thessalonians 5:11 says we should *"exhort one another and build each other up."* In both of these scriptures, the origin of the words "encourage" and "exhort" comes from the concept "to build." The idea is much like a contractor who builds a house. He wouldn't build without a plan, but instead calculates, measures and sets his steps according to codes. When you build a house of encouragement, you begin with a solid foundation—the Father—and a code—the Word. Then as 1 Thessalonians 2 states, you follow "step-by-step" to the finished product.

Our goal is that our children will "live well before God." To reach that goal we have to create a plan and live it out with purpose or intention. Our intent of creating a home of encouragement isn't just about having a "feel-good" place to live, or somewhere everyone is pleasant to one another. Our goal is that the love of God flows through those walls, through our con-

> **Creating a home of encouragement isn't just about having a 'feel good' place to live.**

versations, through every interaction so that He is evident in and through their lives. Ultimately we want to build a character where these skills are used to build up the family of God outside of our walls.

Encouragement doesn't always come in a package of "sunshine." There will be times when our encouragement needs to be given through discipline. Not long ago, Emma was struggling with how she was responding to Kevin and me (Tracie). We began the day with peaceful, subtle nudges—holding her hand and whispering encouragement—to remind her of our expectations for how we speak to each other in our home. As the day progressed the nudges turned into boundaries being made and consequences laid out. By the end of the day the boundary had been crossed and the consequences were given; which made an unhappy child for a short time.

Once emotions settled, we went back to "whispering encouragement" to her. The day ended with a calm discussion regarding our discipline. We explained to her the reason discipline had to happen—our goal being that someday she speaks love to her spouse, her children, her neighbors. Our goal is that her words will build up those around her and shed God's love and light in her world. If we don't portray this, practice this, and require this character trait in our children, it will not happen when they leave our home.

Hebrews 12:11 states, "No discipline seems pleasant at the time, but painful. Later on, however, it produces a harvest of righteousness and peace for those who have been trained by it." With intention we have an end in mind: that our children "live well before God." Throughout their time in our homes, we will use many ways to pursue this objective. Most will be peaceful and whispered, but some will need to come by discernment and discipline. Then the righteousness and peace will come.

When we determine our homes will be built around encouragement and on the solid foundation of God and His Word, then our families can weather the storms of life together. Our children will know that home is a place of refuge and safety, a place with boundaries and discipline. They will also learn how to have a relationship with the Father. So as they grow and begin to build their own homes, His grace and love will be the foundation for generations to come.

Encourage our kids to have their own relationship with God

One of the most important jobs we will have on our parental journey is encouraging our children to run hard after Jesus. We want to be our kids' most enthusiastic cheerleaders as they experience life with God. Our enthusiasm—or lack of it—will have great impact on their desire to know Jesus and follow Him.

I (Elizabeth) recently received a humbling compliment from Taylor. He wrote in a Mother's Day card: "Mom, your constant encouragement and advice is invaluable for a man like me. No matter what I do or when I fail, you never cease to open my eyes and push me back into Jesus' arms." I was broken by this statement as I realized how closely my kids are listening and paying attention to what I'm saying.

Never assume your words are going in one ear and out the other when you are talking to your kids. Their body language may be screaming, "I couldn't care less about this! Please be quiet!" But in reality, a lot more is getting through than you think. Remember, our job as a parent is to consistently redirect them to Jesus when they get off track, have questions, or struggle with doubt or sin.

Our kids are watching to see if Jesus is enough for us, if He's worth giving their life for, and if He is worth serving and loving more than anything else on this earth. This is an overwhelming responsibility, but God is big enough to help us live our lives in a way that will impact our kids for Jesus and cause them to want to serve Him with their own lives.

Our children are looking to us for answers about God. When they are youngsters, we will be the first Jesus they encounter. This is a scary thought, but true: we represent Jesus to them. This doesn't mean we have to live perfectly, but it does mean that Jesus must be recognizable in our lives. As we walk out our lives in Christ before our kids, we want them to look inviting to them. They should be enticed to want to know for themselves this Jesus, who makes Mom and Dad so happy and content. It will be even more important to remain steadfast and trust in Jesus during difficult circumstances so our kids see that Jesus is always enough—not just in good times.

> Our kids are watching to see if Jesus is enough for us, if He's worth giving their life for.

Strange as it may sound, when Sean was laid off from his job in January 2002, it was an answer to prayer. We had been asking God for clear direction for our lives, sensing He was getting ready to change things up a bit. The next year was one of complete dependence on God to provide for our family as we waited for His timing in opening the right door for us.

During this year we experienced miracle after miracle in the area of provision. One that stands out was when we were almost completely out of groceries. After serving a dinner of oatmeal, I had enough food for the kids' breakfast the next morning and to pack a lunch for them, but after that we had nothing left. The kids were well aware of our situation and as a family we were trusting God to provide.

That particular evening I headed over to a girlfriend's house for a visit. Later, as I was leaving, she handed me a card and said she and her husband felt God wanted us to have what was inside. When I got in the car I opened up the card and I found a $100 Walmart gift card. God had provided again in His perfect timing. To celebrate God's goodness, I decided to surprise the kids the next morning with donuts and chocolate milk.

When Taylor came to breakfast and saw the donuts and milk out on the table, he exclaimed, "Where did that come from?" We told him how God had provided and he said, "Mom, when you left last night, I just knew God was going to provide while you were gone." It was so encouraging to see his faith and his thankfulness at God's provision.

That year of complete dependence on God was filled with lessons. One was how important it was for Sean and me to model to Taylor and Elin what trusting God looked like. If we had worried, wrung our hands and fought over money, bills and lack of groceries, our kids would've come away thinking, "Well, I guess God is big enough for the little things, but when it comes to all this big stuff, it's just too much for Him." But instead, by God's grace, we were able to continually point them to Jesus, our Jehovah Jirah, our Provider, and they experienced that God does provide all of our needs, according to His riches in glory (Phil. 4:19).

Part of encouraging our kids to have their own relationship with God is living our faith loudly in front of them. This doesn't mean shouting and cramming it down their throats, but being a living example of faith. It isn't just talking about faith and trusting God, but showing what faith and trust looks like in life. It's much easier for them to believe in God when they see His love, kindness, and faithfulness demonstrated before them. Again, it's not about perfect living, it's about showing the benefits of loving God and trusting Him with your life.

We can encourage our kids to love Jesus from a very young age. One way I (Elizabeth) did this when my kids were just toddlers was by playing praise music in the car, encouraging them to "praise Jesus" by lifting up their hands to Him. Their first experience with praise and worship was not in church, but in the car or at home.

We can also be the first to introduce the Word of God to our kids. What a privilege we have to make the Word come alive as we read the Bible to our children. Making sure our kids always have their own age-appropriate Bible is positive reinforcement for how much we value the Word.

Encouraging them to have their own "quiet time" with the Lord every day begins by having our own times with God each day. As our children witness us reading our Bible and praying, they internalize this critical habit and will hopefully incorporate it into their own lives as they grow older. Sharing what God is revealing to us in our quiet times helps our kids understand the importance of spending time in His presence. They begin to connect the time with God to the wisdom and insight we have about life. As they grow older and establish their own relationship with God, they will understand that a quiet time with God produces guidance and wisdom into their own life.

> As our children witness us reading our Bible and praying, they internalize this critical habit.

My mom has encouraged my relationship with Jesus my whole life. She has consistently fed my spirit by sending me books, subscriptions to great Christian magazines, articles she has read, and CDs of sermons she has heard. Even though I am an adult, she continually encourages me in my walk with the Lord. She has given me an invaluable gift, and I hope to pass along this great heritage to my children and grandchildren.

Here are some steps you can take to begin encouraging your child in his/her relationship with Jesus.

- Let your love for Jesus and your faith in His Word be evident in your life. Make Jesus the hero in your home by giving Him the glory and praise for everything. Show His love to others in front of your kids by serving together at a food kitchen or nursing home.

- Have a regular devotional time together. It doesn't have to be every day, but consistently throughout the week. Find an interesting and age-appropriate devotional book to read together. It's an opportunity to discuss the Bible and answer any questions your kids might have. Don't be afraid of tough questions; you don't have to know it all. If they have a question you don't know the answer to, search out the answer together. This will teach them to dig deeper in the things of God. Make sure your child always has their own, age-appropriate, Bible. A junior high student should not be reading the same Bible he had when he was in third grade. Providing them their own Bible puts great value on it and teaches your kids what a treasure it is. Don't require your child to read their Bible, but pray that God draws them to it like a deer pants after water.

> **Let God's spirit saturate your home in the form of music.**

- Make memorizing Scripture a fun, inviting, family activity. Perhaps talk about and meditate on one verse each week and reward those who put the effort into committing it to memory.

- Let God's Spirit saturate your home in the form of music. Introduce worship music into your family's life as soon as your kids are born. Play it in the car, in the house, on your iPod, put it on their iPods. Let them see you worship God day-in and day-out. Put great value and importance on praising and worshiping God. There is nothing quite like a great song for drawing hearts into His presence.

• As your kids grow into teenagers, take them often to a Christian bookstore and let them choose some great books and devotionals to use. This encourages them to have a quiet time with something other than just their Bible, a companion guide can bring the Bible alive to them and reveal truths they might not see otherwise.

Encourage our kids to be who God has created them to be

In much the same way a contractor prepares his plans, we must do research to meet our objective of building a house of encouragement. In order to be effective in lifting our children up and teaching them who they really are in Christ, we must meet them where they are—knowing their personality and how to best reach them.

Genesis 1:27 says: *"So God created human beings in his own image, in the image of God he created them; male and female he created them."*

Psalm 139:14 says: *"I praise you because I am fearfully and wonderfully made; your works are wonderful, I know that full well."*

This immediately screams "complex!" The idea that our children are made in the image of God makes us view them in wonder—they are a beauty, a miracle, a work of the Father's hand, and as complex and individual as can be!

Those who have two or more children quickly see the diversity and complexity of these creations. God has wired us all a certain way and this personality determines how we respond to life on every level. I (Tracie) am so aware how unique and different in personality are my daughters. The oldest, Ashley, is calm, easygoing, organized, and prepared for any situation. She has become an RN in a pediatric intensive care unit and now she is a mother. My other daughter, Emma, is completely different—full of life, ready to take on anything, and if it involves fast movements and possible scars, so much the better!

Each child is vastly different and they will require different parenting techniques depending on how they are wired. There are multiple resources in books and online to help you discover your child's unique personality traits. Helpful books include *Personality Plus for Parents: Understanding What Makes Your Child Tick* by Florence Littauer and *The Treasure Tree: Helping Kids Understand Their Personality* by Gary and Norma Smalley and John and Cindy Trent. There are also numerous online personality test resources. You can find many links on the Young Ladies Christian Fellowship website at http://ylcf.org/you/personality/. Although this is a website for young ladies, the information and links can be used with our sons as well.

Each child is unique and has their own personality, likes, dislikes, thoughts, and ways of communicating and going about their world. This uniqueness is something to celebrate, and our children need to hear it. The world can be a cruel, criticizing, and oftentimes judgmental place. We want our children leaving our homes each day knowing they are amazing creations of God and with Him they can do anything!

One way to encourage them in this area is by speaking the Word into their lives and reminding them of whose they are and that they are an amazing work of God. Here are a few suggestions:

- Recite scriptures like Genesis 1:27 and Psalm 139:14 to them when they are worried about measuring up to others or comparing themselves to other children.

- Write notes to them about their uniqueness and put them where they will find them unexpectedly, such as in a book they are reading, in a pocket in their back-pack, or in a drawer they frequent.

- Tell them, specifically, the things you love about their uniqueness.

- When it's time, explain their bodies and maturation in a way that shows them how wonderfully they are made. Talk to them about the incredible way God has formed their bodies and how miraculous they are.

Along with these complex children come strengths, weak-nesses, and personality tendencies. It will take some work and investigation, but we need to know these intricacies in-side and out. When we truly understand how these areas play out in our children, we can encourage and guide them to be all they can be for Him. He has given each child gifts that, if we cultivate, water, and weed, He will use to accom-plish amazing things in and through their lives.

Just as it is important for us to recognize our kids' strengths and weaknesses, it's even more important for them to be aware of them. Understanding what they are good at and the qual-ities in their God-given nature helps them have a better grasp on who they are, why they feel the way they do at times, and why they tend to react certain ways to life.

> **Keep your finger on the pulse of your child's self-image.**

A good exercise to help them discover their character strengths and weaknesses is to periodically sit down with them and ask them to write down what they feel are their five greatest strengths and their five greatest weaknesses. This gives an insight into how they are seeing themselves and if they are accurate in their assessment. It allows you to keep your finger on the pulse of your child's self-image.

It's also good to find out how your child receives and gives love. In *The Five Love Languages of Children,* Gary Chapman and Ross Campbell note, "If children feel genuinely loved by their parents, they will be more responsive to parental guidance in all areas of their lives." They characterize this type of love as a "no matter what" kind of love or "unconditional" love—one without strings attached. Finding the love language of our children so we can more effectively communicate with them is a key issue for the foundations of our homes.

The five love languages are quality time, words of affirmation, gifts, acts of service, and physical touch. You can find more information about the languages at: *www.5lovelanguages.com*. Our children may possess more than one language, but most often one predominately stands out.

When we took the "love language" survey to determine our family's unique languages, I (Tracie) learned that Emma had two that were very close, and one that I didn't expect. As I looked back at some of the interactions we'd had in the previous few months and listened closely as we moved forward, I could clearly see how I had been missing the mark. I was not communicating unconditional love to her. I had been communicating in the way I want to be loved. When I began intentionally loving her through quality time, our interactions changed dramatically for the better. It reminded me that our children are longing to receive a "no matter what" kind of love from us that will permeate through all we say and do, to guide and encourage them in their walk.

Another area where we can encourage our children is in their spiritual gifts.

1 Corinthians 12: 4-11 tells us:

"There are different kinds of gifts, but the same Spirit distributes them. There are different kinds of service, but the same Lord. There are different kinds of working, but in all of them and in everyone it is the same God at work. Now to each one the manifestation of the Spirit is given for the common good. To one there is given through the Spirit a message of wisdom, to another a message of knowledge by

means of the same Spirit, to another faith by the same Spir-
it, to another gifts of healing by that one Spirit, to another
miraculous powers, to another prophecy, to another distin-
guishing between spirits, to another speaking in different
kinds of tongues, and to still another the interpretation of
tongues. All these are the work of one and the same Spirit,
and he distributes them to each one, just as he determines."

A spiritual gift is the God-given capacity of every Christian to carry out their function in the body of Christ. In verse 11, we are told that He distributes gifts to each one. This means our children have spiritual gifts and it's our job to help them realize their gift and use it for His kingdom. There are many ways to help your child find their spiritual gift. First, ask the Holy Spirit to help you see the unique ways your child can be a part of the family of God. Watch how they interact within your home, with others, and within the church. Listen for their response to situations and you will begin to see a pattern. There are numerous resources such as books and online surveys to guide you in determining spiritual gifts.

When you begin to sense your child has a particular gift, point it out to them when you see them using it. One time Emma was telling me (Tracie) a story about how badly she felt for a friend on the playground. She told me every detail of the event, how she perceived her friend was feeling, and how she tried to encourage her friend. I told Emma, "I love your heart for others, how soft it is to others' feelings. That is such a gift of encouragement." Believing Emma has the gift of encouragement, I wanted her to begin seeing herself as an encourager. I wanted her to think, "Oh yeah, God just used me in that situation."

This type of thinking helps our children realize God has a plan for them, that He has created them uniquely for His work, and there is a purpose for them here on earth. If this is instilled in our children at an early age, it will be a covering that can protect them from the harsh world outside our homes. When others are unkind, speak ill of them, or treat them as if they don't matter, the Holy Spirit will bring back these conversations and remind them of who God has created them to be.

It is so important to fully understand these principles as all communication and interactions are filtered through our children's personality, love language and spiritual gifts. Before you move on, stop and focus on this area for a while.

- Take a personality test with your child. Begin to read about that personality type so you understand just how God has wired them.

- To find out your child's love language or how they feel loved; ask them to complete this sentence: "When Mom does _____, I feel loved." Then figure out which love language that fits into and begin speaking unconditional love to your children.

- Begin observing your child in different scenarios and interactions to discern their spiritual gifts. Be aware of what excites them or lights them up. Is your child always the one to "think of others first" or offer to serve others? If so, maybe they have the gift of encouragement. Are they compassionate and caring towards others? Maybe they have the gift of a comforter. Be sure you encourage them in their gifts and talk with them about how God can use them in many different ways.

Ensure home is a safe haven

Another step in creating an encouraging environment in our homes is to ensure our children know our homes will always be safe places. They need to know home is where they can be themselves, receive physical and verbal affection, and be encouraged by their biggest cheerleaders. This will look different for each child based on their communication style and personality. For example, the child who has a love language of "quality time" will find it comforting to know you are willing to stop what you are doing and spend undivided time with them to talk or sometimes to "just be." The child whose temperament is a "melancholic" or one who is an introvert needs to know they are safe to speak their fears and disappointments openly to you.

The Word describes God as a place of shelter and refuge from the world. We need to be the tangible example of His safety for our children.

> *"Whoever dwells in the shelter of the Most High will rest in the shadow of the Almighty." (Ps. 91:1).*

> *"It will be a shelter and shade from the heat of the day, and a refuge and hiding place from the storm and rain." (Isa. 4:6).*

Creating a place of safety means allowing our children to "rest" in our shadow, to be "shaded" from the heat of their day, and to have a hiding place from the storms of life. Creating this kind of refuge takes intention. For our homes to be that kind of resting place, we need to build an environment where our children feel safe to communicate the storms they are facing, and express their need for shelter. If our day is fast-paced and full of demands, we might not make the time to really talk about what's going on in our children's lives. If we're always busy and preoccupied with the next task, it will be difficult to actually hear their needs, and we'll miss the opportunity to provide that shelter. We'll also miss a prime time to speak the Word over them, pray with them, and provide guidance and direction.

The home of encouragement allows the characteristics of 1 Thessalonians 2:11-12 to be played out with our children—to hold their hand and whisper words of encouragement. Here are some ways you can be the shelter they need:

- Daily ask the Holy Spirit to help you discern what your child needs from you. Some days this may only be a listening ear; they may not always need to hear your instruction or advice. They many just need to know you are near and available.

- Make sure you are sending the message that they are worthy of your undivided attention. This means to discard all distractions such as TV, cell phones, computer, or music when you are ready to truly listen.

- If they are weathering a storm, and it's their communication style, make yourself the tangible arms of God. Provide more physical touch, hug them, and touch them with affection.

Finally, building a home of encouragement is a process which takes intention and a heart that is open to the guidance of the Father. Remember, it doesn't mean our homes are places where everyone is constantly praising one another and hugging and cheering each other on. It's so much more than that. Encouraging our kids to follow hard after the Lord and make the difficult choices to do the hard things can sometimes be the most challenging of parental duties. We all hate to see our kids walk through valleys and if it were possible, we would go before them and protect them from all the danger. But deep in our souls we know this would not serve them well. How would they ever grow dependent on God if they never truly felt their "need" for Him?

It's in the hard times we feel the "need" for God the most and a house of encouragement is just what our children need to navigate the bumpy road. As we set the foundation, guide our kids step by step, and see them live well before God, we will know we did our job well: we provided them a place of encouragement where they were pointed to the Rock of their salvation and Help in time of trouble (Ps. 18:2).

Reflection Questions:

1. When you think of encouragement, what does that mean to you?

2. How have you encouraged your children to have a relationship with the Father? Which of the suggestions do you think you could start with first?

3. Identify some ways that your child/children is/are unique.

4. What were some of the results from the exercises regarding your child's temperament, love language and spiritual gifts? Were you surprised by the results? If so, how?

5. In what ways do you encourage your children and husband?

6. Do you think your children would say you are an encourager in their lives? Why or why not?

4
A HOME OF HEALTHY COMMUNICATION

"My dear brothers and sisters, take note of this: Everyone should be quick to listen, slow to speak and slow to become angry." — James 1:19

EVERY FAMILY HAS its own communication "style." Whether they are healthy or dysfunctional, we all have patterns and habits we use to communicate within our families. As we establish an atmosphere where ministry can take place, it's important to pay close attention to this critical area.

Every home begins with a man and woman coming together and bringing their own ideas and expectations of what communication looks like. No two homes are exactly alike, so when a couple marries, they soon realize they must find common ground on which to build a house of healthy communication.

This can be challenging to a young couple if one came from a home where raised voices and sarcasm were the norm, and the other came from a quiet home where feelings were kept inside and rarely discussed. Since children usually "adopt" the communication style they experience growing up, what's normal to one person may not be normal at all for another.

I (Elizabeth) realized this one day when my newly adopted sister Denise called me and asked me a very disturbing question. Now twenty-eight, she had experienced a very difficult childhood.

When Denise called, she said, "Liz, Mom just told me Dad has never hit her in their whole married life! Is this true?"

"Well, of course it's true," I replied. "Dad has never hurt Mom."

Then Denise asked, "How many times has Sean hit you?" I was stunned. "Sean has never hit me," I told her, "and if he did, he would be out on the street." It took some convincing, but finally Denise realized that her "normal" was not normal to every family.

Not all stories are as dramatic as this, but the conversation illustrates that there are a lot of different definitions of "normal" out there. A good question to ask ourselves is what will our children consider normal in the area of communication as they leave our home and begin their own?

Encourage our kids to manage their words

The Bible is very clear that words matter. In the King James Version there are 137 verses about the tongue. God knew this would be an area where we would struggle. We cannot construct an environment of encouragement without attending to the words we speak and those we allow to be spoken in our homes. Proverbs 18:21 (MSG) notes , *"Words kill, words give life: they are either poison or fruit: you choose."*

It's our choice whether our words will bring life or death to the spirit of our children. This is an area where we cannot parent with a "do as I say and not as I do" mentality. We have to discipline ourselves to live this principle in front of our children. We need to hold ourselves accountable for what comes out of our mouth and how we communicate to those around us.

Ephesians 4:29 (RSV) says, *"Let no corrupt talk come out of your mouths, but only such as is good for building up, as fits the occasion, that it may give grace to those who hear."* Our goal should be to filter everything we say through the question, "Is this something that will give grace to those who hear?"

Words can quickly destroy the safe environment we are striving to foster. This expectation should strongly be communicated to our children as they interact with each other. All siblings will argue now and then. However, we need to teach our children how to disagree within the boundaries of maintaining an atmosphere of safety and encouragement. Belittling, name-calling, sarcasm, and hurtful words should not be allowed. When we instruct our children to be good communicators, we are setting them up for relationship success outside of our homes, and we are keeping our environment safe. This takes practice and discipline.

> **Words can quickly destroy the safe environment we are striving to foster**

When addressing the words our children choose, we need to encourage them by teaching that Satan is not omniscient like God is. God knows everything—our thoughts, fears, worries, everything about us. The opposite is true for the enemy. He doesn't read our minds and know our thoughts. The only way he knows what is going on with us is by what comes out of our mouth. Our words become either ammunition for him to use against us or they become like fiery arrows aimed at him and his plans.

Because this is true, we must teach our children the power they possess over the enemy by the words that come out of their mouths. It gives a whole new meaning to the phrase "use your words" when they're spoken with the authority of Jesus behind them. For instance, if your child is afraid of thunderstorms, you can teach him that through his words he can drive away the spirit of fear. You could lead your child to repeat 2 Timothy 1:7 and speak it out loud that "God has not given me a spirit of fear, but of power, love and a sound mind, and I command you, Satan, to leave me alone in the name of Jesus!" As a parent, we lead them in speaking these things out loud so our kids learn how to fight the enemy with one of the greatest weapons they have—their words.

Truth must always be considered when we think about the words that are spoken or allowed in our homes. We live in a culture where it appears that our truths have become gray; it's even acceptable to "skew" the truth. When we call it a lie, our culture says it's a "little white lie," but what does that really mean? We must call it what it is: sin. And a lie is a sin. A tweaking of the truth is a sin. An exaggeration of the truth is a sin.

When we allow this trait to slip into our home and children's lives, we give the enemy an open door to set up camp and continue to feed our children lies. The Word says he is the father of lies (John 8: 44) and he will go to great lengths to skew the truth to our children.

The Word is very clear that this is a trait God hates. Proverbs 16:16-19 says, *"There are six things the Lord hates, seven that are detestable to him: haughty eyes, a lying tongue, hands that shed innocent blood, a heart that devises wicked schemes, feet that are quick to rush into evil, a false witness who pours out lies and a person who stirs up dissension in the community."* It really can't get any simpler than that!

Encourage a home filled with good communication

Encouraging our children to communicate well is one of the most important life skills we can give them. Life will be more challenging than necessary if they don't learn how to express their feelings, opinions, and thoughts in a balanced, healthy, and productive manner. Our homes are the training ground for teaching our children how to engage verbally with others in a way that encourages healthy, trustworthy, and honest relationships.

One way to encourage good communication is by allowing your children to have their own voice in your home, reassuring them they will be respected for how they think and feel. We need to validate and respect our children and their feelings. We can't expect our kids to feel good about who they are if we are constantly telling them by words or actions that what they think or feel is not important.

Telling a kid he "shouldn't" feel that way, or "doesn't" feel a certain way does nothing but communicate disrespect. Our children's feelings may not make sense to us sometimes, but disregarding their feelings does not help them, it only hurts them.

I (Elizabeth) was raised in a home where the word "worry" was not used. I never heard my mom say she was worried about something. If I said I was worried, she would always redirect me and encourage me to trust the Lord and not give in to worry. Given my laid-back personality, this was pretty easy for me. As I began to raise my kids, I adopted the same posture towards worry in my parenting. Without realizing it, this attitude of not expressing worry put a lot of pressure on Elin. She had the tendency to worry about things, but she didn't voice those concerns because she felt they were wrong. Instead she pushed all those worrisome thoughts and feelings down inside.

Obviously this caught up with her emotionally. When she was finally free to express her struggle with worry and her hesitation to say anything because of my response, I realized I had done Elin a huge disservice by not allowing her to express how she truly felt. What she needed was a safe place to talk about what she was feeling. She needed assurance that God knew she would sometimes worry, but

He was there to help her cast her anxiety on Him because He cared for her in such a big way (1 Pet. 5:7).

As we give our kids the freedom to voice their thoughts and feelings in our home, we must also erect boundaries. In our house, if I'm in a conversation with one of the kids and their attitude begins to go south, I tell them, "You're about to cross the line." This phrase warns them they had better get control of themselves or consequences will be given. Kids need to know that we will listen as long as their body language, words, and tone of voice stay respectful and honoring towards us as parents.

We set the example of respect and staying in control in difficult conversations. The better we model control and respect, the easier it is for them to do the same. This teaches them that even if we disagree, our love and respect for one another remains intact.

Another aspect in becoming a good communicator is encouraging our kids to be attentive listeners. Having the ability to express our feelings in a respectful and honoring tone is important, but extending the courtesy of a listening ear is an invaluable trait to possess. A good listener asks questions, repeats what they heard, lets the other person finish their sentence, and is not focused on thinking of their response while the other person talks.

Interrupting someone is the epitome of disrespect in communication. Once again, we set the example of what a good listener looks like. I (Elizabeth) admit this is not my strong suit. I really have to pay attention to listening well. I can't tell you how many times my kids have said, "Mom, you are not listening to me, you keep interrupting me." If we want our kids

> **Interrupting someone is the epitome of disrespect.**

to leave our homes with a healthy habit of listening, they must first see it modeled well in our lives.

Here are a few questions to ask about your listening skills:

- Do you allow your child to finish his/her thought when talking?

- Are you thinking about what you're going to say next, instead of listening to what she/he is saying?

- Do you ask questions?

- Do you ever say, "So what I hear you saying is…."

- Do you manipulate with your words?

- Do you tend to "strong-arm" the conversation?

James 1:19 encourages us in the art of listening and communicating well: *"My dear brothers, take note of this: Everyone should be quick to listen, slow to speak and slow to become angry."*

It's important for our children to learn they will not always see eye-to-eye with everyone. It will serve our children well to teach them that everyone comes from different backgrounds, home environments, and life experiences. Home is the place to learn how to handle yourself when you disagree with another person. Just like with listening and voicing our feelings, respect is the key when you find yourself in disagreement with someone.

Some of us don't mind conflict, while others avoid it like the plague. But whatever our comfort level with conflict, we need to learn how to disagree in a God-honoring way. In a home with healthy communication, disagreements don't turn into huge fights. They are opportunities to listen, work together, and come to a resolution—even if that is to "agree to disagree."

I (Elizabeth) always told Taylor and Elin they were given to each other by God so they could learn how to treat others. We put strong boundaries and expectations on how they were supposed to treat one another when they disagreed. For example, no name-calling was allowed. The words "idiot," "stupid," "dork," or any other degrading names were never to be used. We also didn't allow any hitting, kicking, or slapping. We wanted to instill in them a respect for each other, and to teach them how to use their words to work through a disagreement.

Recently I found two letters written by Taylor and Elin after a huge fight they'd had when they were elementary-school-age. It was a rough one, and I needed to make a big deal out of the treatment they had doled out to one another. So I had them each write a letter to God, asking for forgiveness for their cruel behavior towards their sister/brother, and then one to the other, asking for forgiveness.

These letters were priceless as I reread them. Each child expressed how much they loved the other and how important they were to one another. The letter to God was also very precious as they both told the Lord they needed His help in treating their sibling with kindness. Trust God to lead you in your response to your kids when they trip in the area of communication. He will give you creative ideas to train them how to treat others with love and respect.

> In our homes our kids can practice the art of getting along with others.

Our kids will face difficult relational situations throughout their life. We want them not to fall apart when they come face-to-face with conflict in a relationship, but be able to articulate their thoughts and feelings in a respectful tone, and come to a calm resolution.

We want to teach our children the truth Paul admonishes in Romans 12:18: *"If it is possible, as far as it depends on you, live at peace with everyone."*

While it is not always possible to live at peace with everyone, in our homes our kids can practice the art of getting along with others, as well as exhibiting integrity and respect when faced with a disagreement.

In our busy lives we often communicate on the fly, barely thinking or filtering what is coming out of our mouth. We speak in haste about the day's events, list the activities for the family, direct our kids around the house, offer an "I'll pray about that" to our neighbors, and barely acknowledge our spouse in the midst. Creating a home environment where healthy communication thrives is a huge task that takes forethought, discipline, humility, and much prayer.

God is calling us to be cautious and thoughtful communicators. We are to be models where we acknowledge the power of our words, provide an environment where listening is given priority, and value the opinion and thoughts of others. As parents, we are training and guiding our children to be godly communicators with their spouse and children and create a heritage that will be passed down to many generations. A home with healthy communication is the call of Deuteronomy 6:7 (NASB): *"You shall teach them diligently to your children, and shall talk of them when you sit in your house, when you walk by the way, when you lie down, and when you rise up."*

Reflection Questions

1. What did you pick up—positive or negative—about communication while growing up in your home?

2. What attributes would you like to add to your communication style? For example: smile more, change your tone of voice?

3. What would you like to remove from your communication style?

4. What are some of the rules in your home regarding "managing words?" Is there anything new you can implement?

5. Are you a good listener?

6. What improvements can your family begin to make so your home has healthier communication?

5
A HOME OF HUMILITY

"Let me give you a new command: Love one another. In the same way I loved you, you love one another. This is how everyone will recognize that you are my disciples, when they see the love you have for each other." — John 13:34-35

THE TRUTHS WE HAVE considered so far will only have impact if they stand on a foundation of humility. If prayer, communication and encouragement aren't built on humility, they won't take root in our lives, or our children's lives.

Humility is critical in two areas of our lives—as parents, and then in having a repentant heart that is willing to forgive and extend grace to others. Humility is at the root of these actions. Repentance, forgiveness and grace must be practiced on a regular basis if our homes are to be places where ministry can flourish.

Let's be honest, when most of us became parents we had no clue what we were getting into. No one could prepare us for that moment when we laid our eyes upon our child for the first time. The love that flooded into our heart was like nothing we had ever known. In an instant we found ourselves willing to give our life for this little person we had only just met. It is a love that cannot be described, only experienced.

This love drives us to do all we can to be good parents. But what does that look like in today's culture? Parents can feel overwhelming pressure to make sure their kids are getting all the opportunities every other child has. We want our kids to have the best education and be at the top of their class. In sports, we push our children to be the biggest and best—oftentimes putting pressure on them to exceed their own natural abilities. We strip the fun out of playing the game as it becomes all about winning and getting noticed.

> **Parents can feel overwhelming pressure to make sure their kids are getting all the opportunities every other child has.**

We enroll our kids in everything from piano lessons to karate, to soccer, to art class; we're afraid if we don't give them a well-rounded experience, they will somehow fall short when it comes to measuring up to other kids.

Then we compare our kids' behavior to others. We look down on parents whose child is throwing a fit in the grocery store. We think to ourselves, "Get control!" We judge the parents of the teen who is out of control and think, "I wonder what they did to cause their teen to act out like that? Probably didn't spend enough quality time with them." We condemn the parents whose teenage daughter finds herself pregnant with thoughts like, "Well, if her father had 'dated' his little girl, perhaps she wouldn't have given herself away. Thank God my daughter would never act like that."

God forgive us for the sometimes prideful, arrogant, and harsh condition of our hearts. Where is the mercy? Where is the grace? Why are we so quick to point a finger or judge a situation when we have very few facts? Could it be that deep inside, we are afraid? Afraid of looking like a "bad" parent if our kid acts in a disdainful manner, or is last in his/her class academically, or is the uncoordinated one on the soccer field instead of the talented one who always receives the glory? At times, such kinds of fear can drive our parenting. We don't want to look like bad parents so we push our kids to "do good" and to "be good."

I (Tracie) hate to admit I am wrong. I don't like it when I am, and I really don't like it when someone else points it out. I hate it so much that at times, I feel like I'm an expert at justifying and rationalizing. Nor do I like to admit I need help of any kind. I want others, including my family, to feel as though I have it all together—that I'm perfect. Not just in one area but in it all areas—my marriage, parenting, walking with the Lord.

The root of this type of thinking is pride, and it has not served me well over the years. At times, I have been unbending, have hurt others, and have even put my arm out to push God and others away. Pride is part of our human nature. We can trace it all the way back to Eve. She, too, was caught up in the lie that she knew better than God, that she could justify and rationalize her actions. She convinced herself—and, ultimately, Adam—that her way was better and then discredited the words of God Himself!

What does all this talk of pride have to do with ministry in our homes? Plenty, as this attitude can be a huge roadblock to creating an environment of humility and ministry. Humility and pride cannot cohabit. So we have to acknowledge pride before we can really work on repentance and forgiveness. The scripture is very clear about pride; God doesn't like it and it will be our destruction if we don't change. If this is an area where you struggle, take a moment and think on these scriptures:

- *"Pride goes before destruction, a haughty spirit before a fall"* (Proverbs 16:18).

- *"When pride comes, then comes disgrace, but with humility comes wisdom"* (Proverbs 11:2).

- *"Before his downfall a man's heart is proud, but humility comes before honor"* (Proverbs 18:12, TNIV).

You'll notice in these verses that pride will bring a fall but humility will draw us closer to the wisdom of the Father. As parents, isn't wisdom what we need? That means we must have a heart of humility. This will take a work of the Holy Spirit where we have to be receptive to His gentle nudge.

Ultimately we want our children to have a heart of humility which is evidenced by repentance and forgiveness. If this is our desire, then we have to be willing to demonstrate these characteristics to them and within other relationships so they can see what these skills look like.

God does not want us to do anything out of fear or arrogance, especially our task of parenting. He wants us to parent our children with hearts full of His wisdom and humility. It doesn't matter to God if our kids don't act perfect all the time, if she isn't Mozart by the age of ten, or if his ACT score is sixteen. The

> God does not want us to do anything out of fear or arrogance, especially our task of parenting.

question we should ask is, how does God define success in parenting? What is most important to Him? What does He want from us as we raise our children?

Such questions that come from a place of humility help us recognize we simply do not have what it takes to raise our kids on our own. What matters to God is the condition of our child's heart and whether that heart belongs to Him. The most important job we will ever do as a parent is prepare our kids for eternity. In order to do this, we must be on our face before God Almighty, seeking His guidance in all we do as parents, not caring about what others think, but trusting God to lead our kids on the path He chooses for them (Prov. 29:25). This is parenting with humility.

Our children will be greatly affected by our example of humility. They are watching and listening as we go about our lives. Sometimes they catch more by watching us live than by what we intentionally try to teach them.

Teaching the Need for Repentance

Before we can talk about what repentance looks like in our homes, we need to establish why it's important. Why would we need to repent or teach our children to repent? The answer is simple. We repent because we have committed a sin, which disconnects us from God.

The word "sin" is not a popular one in our culture. It's not politically correct. It's too harsh. We feel the need to soften it up a little by calling it "a bad choice." We may avoid calling anything "sin" when in reality, that is exactly what it is. We may chastise our kids for "making a bad choice" when they lie, instead of sitting them down and explaining what they just did was sin and making sure they understand they need to repent and receive forgiveness. The difference between a "sin" and "a bad choice" is that one needs forgiveness and one doesn't.

If our children don't learn what sin is, they won't understand why it's so serious (Rom. 3:23, 6:23). They won't understand how it separates us from God (Isa. 59:2). They won't understand that sin is what the enemy uses to draw us away from God and His Holy Spirit. If we water it down and make it seem less than what it is, we do our children a great disservice. It's not about making them feel guilty or ashamed, it's about making them aware of their

> If our children don't learn what sin is, they won't understand why it's so serious.

sin nature and their need for a Savior (Rom. 7:21-25). It's about helping them understand that they will fall down because they aren't perfect, but when they do sin, Jesus is there to wash the sin away and restore relationship with them.

When our homes are places where we freely discuss our struggles with sin, they become safe places for our kids to confess their own sin. It's healthy—and establishes a life-long pattern—for them to come to us and talk about their struggles. Our response to them is crucial. If you react to their confession with anger, overwhelming disappointment, yelling, or words that pour guilt and shame onto them, they will likely never come to you again. If you respond to them in love, forgiveness, grace and understanding, then you will establish a level of trust with your children that will last into their adult life.

My husband and I (Elizabeth) have seen this firsthand as both our kids have moved into young adulthood, but still come to us for prayer over a particular sin struggle. They know we will stand with them and pray with them and if they want, help keep them accountable.

One time when Taylor was in high school, I was driving him to a doctor's appointment when he said, "Mom, I need you to pray with me about my struggle with cursing. I know it's not right, but I find myself wanting to fit in and using language I know I shouldn't." We talked about why he felt the need to use language like those around him and how it takes more intelligence not to curse than to use foul language. I told him I would be praying for him and then for a long time after that I occasionally asked him about it, keeping him accountable.

Another time Taylor came to Sean and me and confessed a sin. He had already made things right with God, but knew God was asking him to tell us what had happened. When I asked Taylor recently how he felt when he knew he needed to tell us about this particular sin, he said, "I knew you and Dad would be disappointed, but I also knew you would forgive me and not be mad at me." I asked, "How did you know we would respond like that?" He replied, "Because I watch how you and Dad live your lives, and you always told me there was nothing I could do to lose your love. I saw you forgive me for other things, and knew you would forgive me for this, as well."

It's certainly not fun to have our kids confess sin to us. The words, "Mom and Dad, I need to talk to you" can strike immediate dread in our hearts, but when we consider the long-term goal, we should want our children to feel safe to come to us. We should want them to know they will receive love, grace, and forgiveness from us.

Confession is always an opportunity for ministry to take place between you and your child. What greater joy is there to see your child respond to God's prompting and seek forgiveness? What greater joy is there than to take your child's hand and lead them in prayer, thank-

Create an environment where your kids know it is safe to admit their sin.

ing God for His unrelenting grace and mercy? You can't create moments like that on your own, but you can create an environment where your kids know it is safe to admit their sin. It may sound funny, but this is a wonderful thing to experience. It's wonderful because their confession of sin helps you realize your child is listening and responding to the Holy Spirit. As parents, we get to declare 3 John 1:4: "I have no greater joy than to hear that my children are walking in the truth."

So how do we create this environment where open communication and honesty flows? We must first get out of the way and rid ourselves of a heart full of fear or pride. We must allow God to create in us a new spirit of humility and compassion toward those in our homes.

A Heart of Repentance

Repentance is a heavy word that is often used in Christian circles, but it's not clear how many of us fully understand its meaning. Repentance isn't just feeling sorry that we have wronged someone or made a sinful choice. Repentance takes a mindful act of thinking about our actions, feeling regret for them, and making an honest attempt to not repeat them. In short, it's an acknowledgment of our sin, a turn from that sin, and moving toward right-living. It's agreeing with the way God wants us to live.

Since we are human, we will sin against our spouse, children and others. Romans 3:10 states, *"There is no one righteous, not even one."* We have a sinful nature that we must daily place before the Lord, and ask for guidance and assistance in keeping it in check. In *Real Marriage*, Mark Driscoll asks, "None of us likes the consequences of our sin but do we really hate sin? Do we fight against it, wage war against it, put it to death through the power of the Holy Spirit?"

We need to acknowledge and remind ourselves that sin separates us from God. That is ultimately why Jesus came to earth—to restore our relationship with our heavenly Father, so the heart of repentance is necessary to restore our relationship with the Father.

John 3:16 says, *"For God so loved the world that he gave his one and only Son, that whoever believes in him shall not perish but have eternal life."*

We need to realize that every sin affects our relationship with God and with others.

Romans 5:8-10 says, *"But God demonstrates His own love toward us, in that while we were still sinners, Christ died for us. Much more then, having now been justified by His blood, we shall be saved from wrath thorough Him."*

We are going to sin. We are going to make mistakes in our parenting and in our interactions within our family. But Romans 2:4 tells us that *"God's kindness leads us to repentance."* The Holy Spirit can be our guide in these situations and our mistakes can become a beautiful teaching moment. The key is to be open to the prompting of the Holy Spirit and to act upon His leading.

Here are a couple of examples of how I (Tracie) have seen this at work in my life:

Emma and I were having lunch with a friend. The adults began talking about a particular couple and how they were having difficulty in their marriage. Although I knew I should stop the conversation, I continued until we had shared information that was purely gossip. As Emma and I drove away, I felt unsettled about the conversation and felt the Holy Spirit prompt me to repent, and point it out to Emma. I quickly asked God to forgive me of gossiping and for not being a good model for my daughter.

It took me a few miles of quarreling with the Holy Spirit before I reluctantly said to Emma, "You know how we were talking about the couple? Well, that was gossip and God doesn't like it. I have asked Him to forgive me, and I know He has, but I want you to know that I'm sorry. I want you to know that I was wrong and that was not a good example."

I then proceeded to talk with Emma about how even a conversation that started out with good intentions about asking for prayer quickly moved into gossiping, and it was wrong. This was a difficult thing for a woman who doesn't like to admit she's wrong, but I wanted Emma to see the importance of open communication about our sins and how God will quickly forgive if we ask.

Another time when I was disciplining Emma, I completely lost my cool. Before I could catch myself, I said things to her that were not necessary, and most likely hurtful. I sent her to her room and immediately the Holy Spirit brought my anger to my attention, as well as this scripture: "Be quick to hear and slow to speak and slow to anger, for anger does not produce the righteousness of God" (Jas. 1:19). He also prompted me with Ecclesiastes 7:9: "Do not be quickly provoked in your spirit, for anger resides in the lap of fools." Well, what do you do with that? You humbly ask your child for her forgiveness.

After I asked the Lord for guidance with my words, I went to Emma and apologized for my actions and asked her to forgive me. I acknowledged that I was wrong to get angry and say things that were hurtful and unnecessary. I wanted her to know that we all make mistakes, but that God is quick to forgive, and that we would be in our home, as well. It was difficult not to make justifications to her such as, "You shouldn't talk to me that way because it makes me angry," or, "When you respond to me in this way, it makes me mad," or, "If you wouldn't do this, then I wouldn't get so angry." But those statements would have revealed that I was not really taking responsibility for my own actions, and I wanted her to know my actions and responses are choices I must make and take responsibility for every day.

When we are open to the Holy Spirit's prompting, we can:

- Quickly demonstrate a heart of repentance.
- Acknowledge the sin and call it what it is (pride, anger, jealousy, gossip).
- Communicate clearly to those affected.
- Ask for forgiveness.
- Make a decision and ask God for His help to hate sin, and wage war against it in order to make a true, lasting change.

That is why we continually need to give the Holy Spirit room and time to move in our hearts and through our actions. This is so difficult in heated or emotionally driven situations, but God promises us that He will show up and assist us every time we call His name.

We never want to come across to our children as though we have it all together. We have both made our fair share of mistakes and will continue to do so. In fact, we have often asked ourselves why we were writing this book with all the mistakes we've made, but God continues to assure us He does not need our perfection, just our willingness.

And He can turn even the most difficult situations into teaching moments. One time, I (Elizabeth) completely lost control of my emotions with Elin. But as God does,

He stepped in and used it in a profound way to demonstrate what true repentance looks like.

One evening Elin was in need of an attitude adjustment in the worst way, and I was in the middle of conveying this very truth to her when I heard her mumble under her breath, "This is why I wish I could run away." I lost it. I screamed, "If you think you can find it better out there, pack a freaking bag and go!" Ugh.

Elin stormed out the front door. Sean came running from the basement after hearing me scream. He found me fuming in the kitchen, pacing back and forth. I told him what had happened and he went to look out the window. Elin was sitting on our front steps, crying.

After a little while, we heard Elin come in the front door. She came into the kitchen and asked through her tears, "Can I say something?" We told her she could. She said, "I only heard one word as I was sitting out there, and that word was 'repent.' I am so sorry. Will you forgive me? " My anger immediately melted away, and Sean and I both surrounded her with a huge hug, telling her we forgave her and loved her.

The strange thing is I don't remember apologizing to Elin for screaming at her. When I think back on it, I didn't feel any conviction from the Holy Spirit about doing that. Sometimes our kids need a wake-up call, and I believe that's what this was for Elin. It was a reminder to me that God is always active and moving in our homes. He comes into a very unpleasant situation, and brings conviction where it's needed, and extends grace. The Holy Spirit overtakes the enemy and his plans, and turns the experience into a testimony of God's forgiveness and grace.

Take a moment and meditate on these promises:

- *"When I called, you answered me; you made me bold and stouthearted."* (Ps. 138:3).

- *"... and call upon me in the day of trouble; I will deliver you, and you will honor me."* (Ps. 50:15).

- *"He will call upon me, and I will answer him; I will be with him in trouble, I will deliver him and honor him."* (Ps. 91:15).

We would be remiss not to address how difficult it is to change. Our nature is to sin. Changing any behavior takes prayer, discipline, and at times, an accountability partner. Paul talks about this very thing in Romans and Galatians. So if a disciple of Christ and those who actually witnessed the miracles of Christ were struggling with making the right choices all the time, how much more will we need help?

Romans 7:14-25 tells us:

"We know that the law is spiritual; but I am unspiritual, sold as a slave to sin. I do not understand what I do. For what I want to do I do not do, but what I hate I do. And if I do what I do not want to do, I agree that the law is good. As it is, it is no longer I myself who do it, but it is sin living in me. For I know that good itself does not dwell in me, that is, in my sinful nature. For I have the desire to do what is good, but I cannot carry it out. For I do not do the good I want to do, but the evil I do not want to do—this I keep on doing. Now if I do what I do not want to do, it is no longer I who do it, but it is sin living in me that does it. "So I find this law at work: Although I want to do good, evil is right there with me. For in my inner being I delight in God's law; but I see another law at work in me, waging war against the law of my mind and making me a prisoner of the law of sin at work within me. What a wretched man I am! Who will rescue me from this body that is subject to death? Thanks be to God, who delivers me through Jesus Christ our Lord!"

We can so relate to how Paul is feeling. Sometimes we make the same decisions over and over again, even after determining not to. That is why we need to be completely dependent on the Holy Spirit for guidance in every area of our life.

Galatians 5:16-18 says, *"So I say, walk by the Spirit, and you will not gratify the desires of the flesh. For the flesh desires what is contrary to the Spirit, and the Spirit what is contrary to the flesh. They are in conflict with each other, so that you are not to do whatever you want. But if you are led by the Spirit, you are not under the law."*

Although we may struggle with our own sin; that makes grace so much more amazing!

A Heart of Forgiveness

How many times have you instructed your child to say they were sorry to another child or adult? You may even go so far as making them express why they are sorry to that person. We need to remember that repentance is not just about being sorry; it's about identifying a wrong that we have done, having genuine remorse for the action, and then developing a heart that turns away from that action. Because of Christ's sacrifice, we can't stop at repentance alone—we also need to instruct and model forgiveness as part of the process.

Jesus is our example of forgiveness. Romans 5:9 reminds us, *"While we were sinners, we were reconciled."* Before we even knew to ask for forgiveness, He had already completed the ultimate for us, reconciling us to the Father.

I (Tracie) love how Mark Driscoll teaches about forgiveness in *Real Marriage*. He states that forgiveness is a "gospel issue" when he says:

"... no one has been sinned against more than God. No one has been more wounded, grieved, hurt, betrayed, and mistreated than God. Furthermore, we each have contributed to the pain that God experiences, as all sin is ultimately against God. This means that God could be the most embittered person. Instead, He came as Jesus and took our place to suffer for our sins, pronouncing

forgiveness from the cross."

He goes on to explain that "our forgiveness of *others* has very little, if anything, to do with them. Instead, it has everything to do with God. As an act of worship, we must respond to sinful *others* as God has responded to our sin—with forgiveness."

Not only should we forgive as an action of worship; God instructs us to do so. Matthew 6:14-15 (RSV) reads: *"For if you forgive men for their transgressions, your heavenly father will also forgive you. But if you do not forgive men, then your father will not forgive your transgressions."*

One area that should be addressed here is that forgiveness does not mean there are no consequences to the sin. Forgiveness means that we will not harbor feelings about the act; we will not hold it against the other in the future; we will not hold a grudge. Sin still has consequences, and we have to allow our children to experience those in order for the learning process to take hold. But we are called to love them unconditionally, and honor their request for forgiveness with our words and actions. They need to trust that we will stand beside them, pray with them, help them, and hold them accountable in love for any sin with which they are struggling.

So where does grace come in? Grace is unmerited favor; not receiving the punishment you deserve. Sometimes, our kids just need to receive a bit of grace from us. Isn't that what you are hoping for in your relationship with your spouse and others—a little bit of grace?

An example of this came one day when Emma shared with me (Tracie) about an action she had taken at school. She acted out of anger and did some things that were ungodly and wrong. She shared her feelings and we talked about how to handle a situation like that differently the next time. She had already asked the student concerned to forgive her, and it was settled for them. Initially I felt as though I really needed to teach her a lesson with a punishment at home, but as I sat at my desk, I felt the Holy Spirit suggest that I extend grace to Emma.

As I talked with her about the situation, I told her that I was trying to decide about her punishment. She was very quiet, no doubt dreading what was coming next. I then began to talk with her about grace, and that God had prompted me to extend grace to her in this situation. Seeing that her heart was truly repentant, and she had gone to the other person and taken care of the offense herself, she was now going to get grace at home. As you might imagine, she was thrilled.

This is what our Christian walk should be all about, modeling to our children and to those around us what God has done for us. This is no small feat, and we certainly can't do it in our own strength; we need the Holy Spirit to guide and instruct us throughout every encounter with our children.

Ask God to assist you in the area of parenting your child with repentance, forgiveness, and grace, and then wait with expectation that He will guide you.

Reflect on these passages and ask Him to guide you from this day on:

- *"My sheep listen to my voice and I know them, and they follow me."* (John 10:27).

- *"For those who are led by the Spirit of God are the children of God."* (Rom. 8:14).

- *"And I will ask the Father, and he will give you another Counselor to be with you forever-the Spirit of Truth. The world cannot accept him, because it neither sees him nor knows him. But you know him, for he lives with you and will be in you. I will not leave you as orphans, I will come to you."* (John 14:16-18).

As you've read this chapter:

- Is there any area or issue that you need to address as you begin the process of creating an environment of repentance, forgiveness and grace in your home?

- Is there any fear or pride that you need to go to the Lord about? The first action to creating an environment of humility in our home is to ask God to create that environment in your own heart.

- Is there anyone in your family that you need to repent to and ask forgiveness from? Just like David, ask God to search your heart and show you anything that might hinder that the work He is doing in your home.

Psalm 139:23-24 says:*"Search me, O God, and know my heart; test me and know my anxious thoughts. See if there is any offensive way in me, and lead me in the way everlasting."*

Now, ask the Holy Spirit to guide your words and actions that they may reflect the love of God and assist you in creating a house of humility.

Reflection Questions

1. Do you find yourself comparing your children and their achievements and behavior to other children? If yes, reflect on why that is.

2. Have you ever judged another parent based upon the actions of their child? Consider how God wants us to respond when another person's child makes wrong choices.

3. What kind of an understanding does your child have about the subject of sin? Do you call sin "sin" in your home?

4. Would your child feel free to come admit a sin to you? Would he/she feel safe coming and admitting a sin struggle with you? Why or why not is the comfort level there?

5. Do you struggle with forgiveness or do you tend to be able to forgive easily in most cases?

6. Is it easy or difficult to think of others ahead of yourself? How could you begin to do this?

6

A HOME OF MINISTRY TO OTHERS

"Let me give you a new command: Love one another. In the same way I loved you, you love one another. This is how everyone will recognize that you are my disciples when they see the love you have for each other." — John 13:34-35 (MSG)

JESUS DIDN'T MINCE WORDS when He laid out His expectations of how we should love one another. In the book of John, He gets very specific in explaining His heart.

We should see our homes as training grounds where our kids learn how to love others as we practice loving each other in our family. Love is what drives us to make our homes places of ministry. A ministering family not only touches its own, but all those it touches outside the home, as well.

Our desire is to see homes not just where Jesus is active and alive in us and our children, but to move us to thinking of our families as God's hands, feet, and mouth to spread His love, mercy, and grace to others. Can you imagine the church's tremendous impact if we could just grab hold of God's intention for the family as a powerful force that brings His truth to others?

Teaching our kids to think outside themselves, and be alert and sensitive to others' needs, takes a lot of intention. It will not just happen. We must have a game plan if we want our kids to love others and be comfortable ministering to them.

It's up to us to set the example of what loving others looks like. If our kids witness us caring about other people by praying for them, providing a meal, blessing them financially, or inviting them to dinner, they will be much more likely to care about people, too. They will internalize that life is about spreading God's love to others and not all about them. Our children will be more content, kind, and at ease ministering to those in need.

> It's up to us to set an example of what loving others looks like.

Recently a woman at our church shared with me (Elizabeth) one of her first memories of meeting my family. I have no recollection of this, but evidently she was sharing a prayer request at church, and I suggested we pray together right there. I called over Taylor and Elin, who were about fourteen and eleven years of age, and asked them to join me in praying for my friend. We laid our hands on her and prayed.

My friend had never had someone stop and pray with her right then when she shared a prayer request. Furthermore, she had never had kids lay their hands on her and pray! That moment truly touched her. It goes to show how much impact a simple prayer can have.

This is just one example of how we can bring our kids into a situation and let them witness and be a part of ministering to someone else. The next time someone shares a need with you, why not stop and pray right there with them? And if your kids are around, include them, and as a family touch that person with His love.

If our home is a training ground, it's important we know exactly what we are training our children to do. The goal is to plant the seed of compassion and love in their hearts for other people. So let's talk about how to train our kids to:

- Recognize pain in another person.

- Express empathy for someone.

- Establish a comfort in praying for others.

- Encourage and uplift another person.

- Take God's love and share it outside the home.

Recognize pain in another person

The first step in helping someone is to recognize when they might be hurting. Almost everyone we come into contact with is struggling in some way or knows someone who needs ministry. We ask each other all the time, "How are you?" But do we really want to know the answer? Do others feel free to express their true feelings with us? Our culture is so busy and frenetic that often we ask this question without the slightest real interest in how the person is truly feeling. We miss opportunities all the time because we miss the "cues" that would tell us the person is hurting.

Our only hope is to ask the Holy Spirit to tune us into what He is doing, opening our hearts to listen and obey Him. This skill can be learned in our home simply by being sensitive to those with whom we live. Asking the question, "How are you doing?" with sincerity, and then responding to the Holy Spirit if we sense sadness or pain will teach our children to see with eyes that look inside a person's heart.

Express empathy for someone

The definition of empathy is *the ability to understand and share the feelings of another.* It's not "feeling sorry" for someone, but "feeling with them" in whatever they're going through. An empathetic person helps another person not feel alone in her situation. What a wonderful and calming presence we can be when we learn how to express empathy to another person.

The ability to express empathy comes more naturally to some than to others. I (Elizabeth) happen to be the kind of person who has to "work at" being empathetic. As a mom, this has been a real struggle for me. One of my pet peeves is when someone gets easily offended or wears a big chip on their shoulder. I'm more of a "get over it" kind of gal—but I have to say that hasn't worked too well for me when dealing with my kids!

I have realized—slowly, I might add—that, no matter their age, my kids need me to listen and empathize with them when they are hurt. They don't need me to point out what they might have done wrong, or tell them to get over it and let it go, or suggest they go make it right. They need me to tell them I understand and am sorry for their hurt. They need physical affection and comfort from me. This empathy tells them they are not alone and that someone else knows how they are feeling and better yet, feels it with them.

> Empathy tells them they are not alone and that someone else knows how they are feeling.

So our kids learn this quality by experiencing it from us. When we have empathy for our children, they sense we "feel" what they are feeling and they will, in return, be able to more easily share in the feelings of others.

Establish a comfort in praying for others

It is so important to establish a comfort level in our kids' lives for praying with another person.

When we pray for another person, God just automatically shows up and touches them. It's not us, it's totally Him. It may require our willingness, but it is His faithfulness that comes and brings peace to the person's heart, no matter how anxious they are.

One time when I (Elizabeth) was working as a receptionist at a doctor's office, a patient called in and said she couldn't breathe well and would not be making her appointment because she had just called 911 and was waiting beside the road for the ambulance. I could hear a child crying in the background and the woman was beginning to get really upset.

I told her it was going to be okay and asked if I could pray with her. She said, "Oh, yes, please!" As I prayed, God was faithful and His presence entered her car and calmed the crying baby and brought peace. The next day the woman showed up at the office asking for me. She wanted to thank me for praying with her, and to tell me how much it had meant. It was a simple prayer, but God used it in a much bigger way than I could ever have imagined.

There were many times when I had an opportunity to pray with patients over the phone. Sometimes I took the opportunity, but at other times though I knew God was asking me to pray, I ignored His prompting. I regret all those times when I was too afraid or embarrassed to step out in faith. It only resulted in missed opportunities.

In our home, the responsibility of prayer needs to be a shared effort. There should be opportunities at every turn for our kids to pray for their siblings, the dog, over a meal, and for us. No one person should be the only "prayer warrior" in the family. When someone doesn't feel well, gather the family around and lay hands on him (Luke 4:40) and have each child say a prayer of healing. If the dog is sick, gather around and pray over it. At meal time, allow kids to take turns praying for the food. You could add a prayer request for someone else at each dinner prayer to encourage empathy for others.

Home is the safe place for you and your children to practice and get more comfortable with prayer. By giving your kids opportunities to pray at home, they will become comfortable with praying for others. It will be more natural to pray with someone outside the home if they are already used to praying over you.

There is great joy in witnessing your child minister through prayer to someone. Recently I saw Taylor reach out to an older man who had come over to our house. This man struggles in a lot of ways, and before he left, I overheard Taylor ask him if he could pray with him. As I gave them some privacy, I looked back and saw my son put his hand on this man's shoulder and share God's love with him through prayer.

Encourage and uplift another person

In the New Testament, Paul continually exhorts his fellow believers to love, serve, and encourage one another. Listed below are just a few of these exhortations.

- *"Be completely humble and gentle; be patient, bearing with one another in love."* (Eph. 4:2).

- *"You, my brothers and sisters, were called to be free. But do not use your freedom to indulge the flesh; rather serve one another in love."* (Gal. 5:13).

- *"Finally, brothers and sister, rejoice! Strive for full restoration, encourage one another, be of one mind, live in peace. And the God of love and peace will be with you."* (2 Cor. 13:11).

We can use these passages to help our kids understand that God's heart is all about us living a life that uplifts and encourages others. We demonstrate this by getting along well with others, not gossiping and complaining about others, and being positive about other people.

The right attitude towards other people will radically affect your children. You may know mothers who talk negatively about other people around their kids, and if so you will probably have noticed that their kids do exactly same thing. You can tell when it's a habit in the family to discuss irritations or frustrations about others. This is such an unhealthy habit to establish with our kids.

Our kids should only hear us speak uplifting words about others, with empathy, and giving folks the benefit of the doubt when we hear about bad behavior. This helps protect our family from a judgmental and critical spirit, and once again, our kids will "catch on" how to live lovingly with others.

Encouraging those in our families is very important, as well. One way to develop this habit is during dinner. Have each person go around the table and say one kind thing about each person. This puts the emphasis on our strengths and uplifts those we love the most. When our kids feel good about who they are and know their family loves them, they will be more likely to be a person who is uplifting to others, instead of negative and critical.

Take God's love and share it outside the home

We want our kids to feel as though they have something to offer other people. As we train them to recognize pain, express empathy, pray with others, and be encouraging, God will open up opportunities for them to minister outside their home. We want to prepare and encourage them for whenever those opportunities arise.

One summer, I (Elizabeth) taught a swim class that included my seven-year-old nephew, Tony. I was standing outside the pool trying to demonstrate a stroke technique, but my neck was very stiff that day and I had limited movement. I told the kids I was sorry, but I couldn't show them very well what the stroke looked like because my neck was so sore. Tony spoke up and asked, "Aunt Liz, would you like me to pray for your neck?"

My first reaction was to dismiss his offer. But then I stopped myself, and said, "Thank you Tony, I would love that." He came over to the side of the pool and as I knelt down, he laid his hand on my neck. He prayed: "Jesus, please touch Aunt Liz's neck. Please Jesus, take all the pain away. Thank you, Jesus."

About five minutes later, I made a motion and realized my neck was no longer hurting. In fact, I had full movement and there was no pain whatsoever. I yelled out as I moved my head all around, "Hey Tony, look! My neck is healed!" His response was simply, "That's great Aunt Liz!"

After the lesson, I told my sister what had happened. She told me that she couldn't even take an Advil without Tony asking her if he could pray for her. Why does this child feel so comfortable with ministering to his mom or his aunt? Because his *home* has been a training ground where he has witnessed what it looks like to pray, uplift, and care about another human being. And now he is taking it outside his home.

Open for God to be seen by others

Not only are our homes training grounds, they are places where God's love can touch all who enter. His Word encourages us to be a "light" so others will see Him and glorify Him. Matthew 5:14-16 states: *"You are the light of the world. A town built on a hill cannot be hidden. Neither do people light a lamp and put it under a bowl. Instead they put it on its stand, and it gives light to everyone in the house. In the same way, let your light shine before others, that they may see your good deeds and glorify your Father in heaven."*

Did you catch that? Our light—God shining through us—is to shine on everyone in the house... family, friends, neighbors. As others spend time in our homes, they will begin to be drawn to His spirit. A pastor we know encourages his congregation to "make your life an invitation to come and see." Through our actions, others will see a tangible example of Christ's love. If they don't know Him personally, our lives may be the very thing that pique their interest to check this "God" thing out. So how do we let our light shine within our homes and allow God to reveal himself to those who are there?

Act the same when guests are in our home

Consistency is so important for us and our children. If we act differently when guests are in our home, we send a message that our beliefs are something to hide or that we are embarrassed by them. Proverbs 29:25 (MSG) says that *"fear of human opinion disables; trusting in God protects you from that."* We ultimately want our children to minister to others inside and outside our homes. We must always be aware that those who enter our homes may be hurting, need love, or need God's grace. Most importantly, we need to create an environment where we can share the Healer, Counselor, Creator, and Lover of our souls. So what does this look like in everyday life?

In our home, I (Tracie) often have Christian music playing, and we don't turn it off when we have guests. We always say a blessing at the dinner table. If the occasion arises for God to be praised, I may give a quick, "Thank you, Jesus!" Or if prayer is needed, I'll say, "Jesus, help us," or ask if I can pray for whoever needs help. Such actions send a consistent message to my kids and all who enter our home that God is the center and head of our family. This takes intention, but when we ask the Holy Spirit to guide and direct every word, action, and thought, it allows God the opportunity to work through us to touch those in need.

> Treat everyone who visits like family.

Treat guests like family

Another way for God to make Himself known is by creating an environment where we treat everyone who visits like family. The grace, mercy, forgiveness, and compassion that family members extend to one another should also be extended to those who come into our homes so that God can reveal His very character through us.

When guests visit our home I (Tracie) have arranged things so that they are greeted at the "doorposts" (Deut. 6:9) with a plaque that reads, "Peace and grace to all who enter this place." I want this blessing to be on anyone who enters... kids included. Once they are in, they are "family" and we treat them like it at all times.

My home has scriptures, messages of encouragement, and personal messages placed in each room. When guests arrive, I usually write a "welcome" message and scripture on a large plate, and put it on a stand in the kitchen. This plate has become a point of discussion and curiosity to those who visit often. Friends are always keen to see what I write on the plate. It can be a quote from the weekly teaching at our church, a scripture, or just a message. I love it when my kids light up from a message written especially to them, or a neighbor feels blessed by the words, or friends are challenged from the teaching!

Since Kevin is in the Marines, many of our guests are military families. We always offer our table, bed, and family as a surrogate for those far from home. At times this has meant sharing a holiday table and traditions. Each November, I put out a bowl of small pieces of paper with pens and instruction to all who visit to write out something they are thankful for so we can read them at the Thanksgiving table. I truly want everyone who enters to write something. If we have a Marine at the table, I give him a chance to write something, and then we take time to let all of those around the table share. This is followed by a prayer of thanksgiving before we eat. I believe this sends a strong message to all sitting there that we give God all the glory for all of the events during the past year.

When the guests are friends of my girls, I always encourage them to feel at home. While Ashley was a teenager we had girls in and out, spending the night, getting dressed for performances, eating at our table. They became like my second daughters. If I sensed they were troubled or if they shared a need, I would offer my thoughts, remind them what scripture says, or offer to pray for them. I tried to greet and send them off with a warm, affectionate hug and an invitation to come again any time.

Make ourselves available

Another way for us to allow God to be seen in our lives and homes is to be available or open to those around us. This requires a closeness with the Holy Spirit; leaning in to hear His whisper and seeking His direction during interactions with anyone we meet.

> Besides loving Him with all our hearts, loving others is the most important thing we can do.

This is easier for some to do, but God calls all of us to be His representatives in our own mission field. In many Christian circles, missionaries are viewed as those who are "called" into the ministry to love and serve others in impoverished countries. But Jesus didn't define the word "missionary" this way, we did. In the Word, God's desire for our "mission" is very clear: besides loving Him with all our hearts, loving others is the most important thing we can do.

Matthew 22:36-40 states:

"'Teacher, which is the greatest commandment in the Law?' Jesus replied: 'Love the Lord your God with all your heart and with all your soul and with all your mind. This is the first and greatest commandment. And the second is like it: Love your neighbor as yourself. All the Law and the Prophets hang on these two commandments.'"

Philippians 2:3-8 says:

"Do nothing out of selfish ambition or vain conceit. Rath-

er, in humility value others above yourselves, not looking to your own interests but each of you to the interests of the others. In your relationships with one another, have the same mindset as Christ Jesus: Who, being in very nature God, did not consider equality with God something to be used to his own advantage; rather, he made himself nothing by taking the very nature of a servant, being made in human likeness. And being found in appearance as a man, he humbled himself by becoming obedient to death—even death on a cross!"

What does this kind of availability look like?

Even though the number of activities increased as our daughters grew older, our priority of church attendance did not change. Our expectation is that the family is in church together, every Sunday. So when the girls' friends began spending the night with greater frequency, it was natural to invite them along. How fun it was to watch their friends get excited about Jesus and want to come back. There were times when a friend lived across town but wanted so badly to go that we drove across town to get them there.

About two years ago, I realized that many of our neighbors were experiencing situations in their lives where they needed God to intervene. Marriages were rocky, children were straying, relationships were strained, health was declining.

I began feeling burdened to pray for each one. As I started my list and prayed for each person on my street, I felt the Holy Spirit call me to reach out to them. I felt like we should come together and support each other in prayer. I didn't know if anyone would agree with me or come to pray, but I knew my obedience was to offer the time and place. I contacted every neighbor I knew and invited them to begin a prayer group every other week at 6:30 a.m.

Interestingly enough, even those who were not comfortable praying out loud—or maybe had never prayed out loud—came and initially just listened. As time went by, they became more comfortable praying out loud, and now we each take a turn in our circle. A small group continues to meet every other Tuesday to join in prayer for our families and friends. We have seen God answer so many prayers, and we've become such a close group of friends now. Prayer draws us to the Father and to one another.

Kevin and I are in a weekly small group with our church, and we truly love the couples we are "doing life" with. A few summers back, I felt like a few gals in our group wanted to get together over the summer for some connected girl time. Again, I felt the Holy Spirit prompt me to open our home. I decided to invite a very eclectic group—those in our small group, ladies at work, those in the neighborhood, and any of their friends who wanted to come. The list was about thirty names. The response was overwhelming and that began the Summer Book Study that continues to this day. There are some ladies I don't see all year until the study comes around, and then we reconnect.

The phrase "If you build it, they will come" from the movie *Field of Dreams* has proven to be true in our lives, too. People long to be with others and have relationships, but in our busy and chaotic culture, we just don't know how to do it. However, make the opportunity available, and you will see that they come.

One way my Kevin and I "build it" is by pulling the lawn chairs, and sometimes even the fire pit, into our driveway. Soon, one by one our neighbors bring their chairs out and we begin talking. Next, someone goes in to get some munchies or something for the kids. Do we always talk about church and what God is doing in our lives? No. Sometimes it's about building relationships so that over time our lives become the invitation to "come and see." If we are willing and available, He will use us to draw them to Him.

If you are feeling like you don't have the gift of hospitality, try to reconfigure your idea of what it means. God calls us to love everyone, take care of the orphans and the widows, and share life with anyone, including our enemies. Just ask God to show you where you can reach out and love on those around you.

You could start right now. Go outside and sit in your driveway, on your porch, or even stand on your sidewalk, and ask God to show you how you can begin loving others right there in your neighborhood.

Provide opportunities to serve together

Acts 1:7-8 says: *"It is not for you to know the times or dates the Father has set by his own authority. But you will receive power when the Holy Spirit comes on you; and you will be my witnesses in Jerusalem, and in all Judea and Samaria, and to the ends of the earth."*

When Jesus instructed His disciples with these words, He was talking about touching your neighborhood first, then your community, then further away. This means we are all in full-time ministry, just exactly where we find ourselves today. You, too, have a mission field in your neighborhood, workplace, or moms group. He has placed us at this very time in this very place to be used for His glory.

I (Tracie) am part of a church that has small groups which participate in four, twelve-week sessions a year. As part of each session, our group tries to do some type of community service, to be the church outside the walls. We make sure that each of these service days includes all of our kids. I love these events because our children get to truly see the joy in serving. As our group gathers at the location, prays and gets started, our children see us laughing and enjoying fellowship as we work. They learn that serving God and others makes our heart glad—and His heart, too.

A few years ago Kevin and I felt like we should incorporate a family service project into our monthly activities. This wasn't just for our children, but for us, as well. We all need a reminder to think outside of ourselves and look for opportunities to serve others who are in need. We found a small non-profit group called Fill-A-Belly and began to volunteer once a month, helping with meal preparation and service and fellowshipping with those who came. This was an amazing experience for our entire family. Our daughter, Emma, became close to a single mother and her two children, and while the kids played games before their meal, my husband and I would talk with the mom and ask her how we could pray for her. We all learned how to empathize, love, and serve others just as we are commanded.

Another time of growth for our family was when Kevin agreed to mentor a sixteen-year-old young man. This boy had been in and out of foster homes most of his life. He struggled with feeling abandoned and that no one cared about him. He and Kevin immediately bonded. One of their areas of common interest was construction, so they joined Habitat for Humanity as part of their weekly time together.

As time went on, our family became fond of this young man and truly enjoyed sharing a "family" experience with him in our home, at our table, and in our community. Did he ever come to church with us? No. But God uses our willingness to change the trajectory of others' lives; my prayer is that we planted the seed of God's love in that young man's life and that others have now watered and fertilized it so that someday he will have a breakthrough to his own relationship with Christ. Our job was to be obedient, love on him—even when he was not so loveable—and allow God to use us to show His love, compassion, and forgiveness to a hurting young man.

Invite others to become part of the family

It's one thing to be ready for our homes and families to be used for ministry to others as they visit, but consider being willing to take an even bigger step. We believe our homes should not only be places of ministry for our own families, but for whomever God wants to bring into them. It pleases God when we answer His call and open our hearts and homes to those He wants to live with us, even if only for a season.

Growing up, I (Elizabeth) saw my parents open our home in a variety of different ways to other people. I can remember a little boy named Louis coming to our house on holidays, when I was a little girl. Louis lived in a children's home in town but on Christmas and Easter, he would stay with us and become part of our family. We treated him like one of our own.

When I was a teenager, my parents opened our home to unwed mothers. They did this to put action behind their support for the pro-life movement. We had four young women live with us at different times, and we loved them and welcomed them for those difficult months of their lives. This impacted me tremendously as each of these girls became my "sister" for the duration of their stay.

When I was in college, my parents invited a foreign exchange student from Germany into their home and later became foster parents for a few years. After I married, they would invite young college kids to stay in their home. Recently they invited a single gal who is getting her degree in social work to live with them. I can't think of a time when my folks didn't have someone living with them.

Because my parents live with this open-heart mentality, God has blessed our family beyond our wildest imagination. Denise was a young woman who attended my parent's church when her landlord suddenly called her lease. My folks invited her to live with them for a couple of months while she found another place.

During her stay, they learned Denise had no family to speak of, as she had been taken out of an abusive home as a teenager and put into foster care. Those two months with our family turned into two years, at the end of which God had woven Denise into our family in such a way that my parents legally adopted her at the age of twenty-eight. They got a fifth child and my siblings and I got another sister.

As a result of the environment in my parents' home, the heart of my parents filtered into their children. Denise and her husband have adopted four children over the past eight years. My brother and his wife adopted a little boy from Ethiopia. Sean and I have had a foreign exchange student from South Korea living with us for three years. My sister and her husband look after a gentleman who has disabilities and needs help in life. And my other brother and his wife have helped and befriended many older folks in their community.

You may not have been thinking about your family in the light of ministry before reading this chapter. Our prayer is that you begin to be intentional about your mission as a family. What is God calling you and your family to do? What kind of impact can your family have?

God has assignments for your family all picked out and ready to go, so what are you waiting for? Let's do it!

Reflection Questions

1. Have you ever looked at your home as a training ground? What do you think of that analogy?

2. What do you think of the idea that your family is a powerful force in God's hands to impact the world around you? Have you ever thought of your family in these terms?

3. What ideas can you come up with to be more effective in teaching your kids about expressing empathy for others or encouraging and uplifting another person?

4. How do guests who enter your home know that your family are followers of Christ?

5. Do you feel your life, time, and home are available for God to use as He pleases? List two to three ways you will try to make yourself and your family more available.

6. What are your feelings about bringing others into your home for a season?

7. What is your mission field?

8. Look for opportunities to allow your children to pray out loud. Where will you start?

FINAL THOUGHTS

Y OU KNOW THAT SAYING, "It takes a village"? This is so true when raising kids to follow hard after Jesus. We cannot parent alone on an island. We need each other so very much. We want to challenge you to find other parents with whom you can encourage and be accountable to as you implement some of the ideas in this book. You are not alone in your feelings of inadequacy. Every parent on the planet has lived with the fear of failing their kids. We have, and we know we couldn't parent without the support and help of others.

As friends, we have supported each other through the most challenging of parenting issues. We love each other's kids like our own. We can't tell you how many times we have called one another asking for prayer for one of our kids or for ourselves as we are in need of God's wisdom in knowing how to handle a situation. We run ideas by each other and ask each other's opinion... we help each other be a better parent.

We want to be one of those resources of encouragement to you and your family. You can find us on the Web at *livingwellministry.com*. At our website you will find information about what we do as Living Well Ministry, as well as our blog and a contact page to email us. We would love to hear from you. If you have prayer requests, we would count it a privilege to pray with you. If you have ideas and comments about what is working in your family in regards to creating a place for everyday ministry, we invite you to share them with us and we will pass them along to our blog readers.

Thank you for joining us in discovering God's heart for your home. He is more than available to help you be the best parent you can be. Parenting well is a huge challenge for us all and you are not alone in your trepidation and desire to "do it right."

Allow your home to become a place where your children will have the opportunity to experience the amazing love and power of Christ Jesus, and then as a family, go share Him with the world.

RESOURCES

Chapman, Gary, Campbell, Ross, *The 5 Love Languages of Children* (Chicago, IL: Northfield Publishing, 2012).

Driscoll, Mark/Grace, *Real Marriage: The Truth About Sex, Friendship & Life Together* (Nashville TN: Thomas Nelson, 2012).

Littauer, Florence, *Personality Plus for Parents: Understanding What Makes Your Child Tick* (Grand Rapids, MI: Baker Publishing Group, 2000).

Trent, John and Cindy, Smalley, Gary and Norma, *The Treasure Tree: Helping Kids Understand Their Personality* (Nashville, TN: Thomas Nelson, 1998).

Young Ladies Christian Fellowship at *http://ylcf.org/you/personality/*.

CONTACT THE AUTHORS

Tracie and Elizabeth offer engaging and transformational teaching on a wide variety of subjects through Living Well Ministry. Whether your plans involve a single day or evening event, or encompass a broader time-frame such as overnight or weekend retreats, we can tailor ministry to fit your specific needs. Tracie and Elizabeth have enjoyed powerful impact as a team, but are also available as individual speakers. They are passionate about and address key subject areas such as :

- Relationship with God
- Marriage
- Parenting
- Lifestyle
- Single Motherhood

To learn more about Living Well Ministry
or to schedule an event, visit their website at:
www.livingwellministry.com

Follow their blog at:
www.livingwellministry.com/blog

CPSIA information can be obtained
at www.ICGtesting.com
Printed in the USA
FSOW02n0029280815
10200FS